Peter Webley

THE POWER IN
Forgiveness

Power that mends, heals and makes new

CONTENTS

Foreword 5

Introduction 9

Chapter 1   Power Belongs to God............................. 11

Chapter 2   No Other Sacrifice 25

Chapter 3   Who is Onesimus?.. 37

Chapter 4   By Example.. 47

Chapter 5   Why is it so Difficult? 61

Chapter 6   Do I Go First? 75

Chapter 7   What's in it For Me?..................................... 87

Chapter 8   What if it's Rejected? 97

Chapter 9   Where Does Love Come
             into Forgiveness?....................................... 105

Chapter 10   All Because He Forgave Me 117

Chapter 11   When Healing Comes 125

FOREWORD

It is my privilege to not only know Peter Webley as a member of my congregation, but also as a very good friend. We have served the Lord together in a variety of ways, from serving on the board of the Bristol City Mission Society to filming promotional ministry videos in Bosnia to, more recently, building our new church and community hub. He has also been a wise source of advice over the years and someone whose both love for and knowledge of scripture is insightful and practical. It was therefore an honour to have been asked to write the foreword to his first book. Many would have sought a high-profile person to do so in order to raise the profile of their work, but that is not Peter. He is someone who only seeks to bring glory to the Lord and this book continues in that desire.

There are certain things that stay in the memory for a lifetime, events that can be both for good or ill, but which shape the person we become, especially in our formative years.

In my early youth I saw the movie *The Hiding Place*, the adaptation of Corrie ten Boom's book of the same name. Corrie was a Dutch watchmaker who during World War 2, along with the other members of her family, lived out their faith in Jesus by hiding Jews from Nazis in their home. After they were betrayed in February 1944 she and her sister Betsie were sent to Ravensbruck Concentration Camp, where Betsie later died.

After the war in 1947, Corrie was preaching in a church in Munich about the forgiveness of God. After the meeting she met one of the former Ravensbruck SS guards who had been particularly cruel towards Betsie. He had since given his life to Christ and sought Corrie's forgiveness. In those moments that seemed to pass like hours Corrie wrestled with the most difficult thing she had to do in her life. Yet with the help of God, she forgave this man.

As a young man of 20 I vividly recall the news footage of a terrible atrocity that occurred on 8th November 1987, Remembrance Sunday, in Enniskillen, a small town in Northern Ireland. The quiet reverence as people gathered for a service intended to honour those lost due to war was shattered at 10.43am when a 40lb IRA bomb exploded near to the town's cenotaph. As a result 63 people were injured and 12 people died.

In the midst of the carnage that was caused by this barbarous act, one man spoke words that flew in the face of the rage and anger that was felt that day. Gordon Wilson, a devout Christian, had witnessed his daughter Marie, a nurse, lose consciousness in the rubble of a collapsed building lying next to him. She later died as the result of her injuries. Interviewed by the BBC he said, 'I bear no ill will, I bear no grudge . . . I will pray for these men tonight and every night.'

On 7th July 2005 another terrorist atrocity took place, this time in London. Four suicide bombers targeted civilians on the London Underground and bus networks, causing the deaths of 52 people in total. One of those was Jennifer Nicholson, a talented musician who was killed on the Circle Line at Edgeware Road by a bomb that had been planted by Mohammad Sidique Khan.

Jenny was the first-born daughter of an Anglican priest, Julie Nicholson, who was the minister of St Aiden's Church in St George, Bristol, the same locality as my own. Julie Nicholson was unable to find it in her heart to offer the same forgiveness that Gordon Wilson did, which ultimately led to her stepping down from ministry. Some ten years later, during an interview with the *Radio Times* she said, 'I can't forgive on behalf of Jennifer, I could only consider forgiveness for the wounds to me as a mother, and those wounds remain raw. So it's not something I'm going to countenance.'

How is it that the response of followers of Jesus, to admittedly terrible acts of evil, can be so different, when we are commanded that *'if you hold anything against anyone, forgive them, so that your Father in heaven may forgive you your sins'* (Mark 11:25)?

In this book, Peter explores some of the reasons why we, even as Christians, find it so hard to forgive, even when we have been forgiven so much ourselves. He looks at the struggles behind our inability to forgive, what prevents us from doing so and how to overcome these, acknowledging that it is often very difficult. He also considers the benefits to both the forgiver and the forgiven.

This is not a theoretical thesis written by an academic, but a practical and pragmatic exploration of the subject matter as Peter writes with candour, sharing from deeply personal experiences in this area.

This book has been written as a resource to help those who are bravely facing the reality of acknowledging that this is an issue in their life and wanting to take the steps necessary to deal with it. By reading this book can I encourage you that you are heading in the right direction. As you read, you may feel that you are too weak to continue, but remember that it is in our weakness that God is able to do His greatest work in our lives. To make the impossible possible for His glory.

Finally, never forget that '*it is for freedom that Christ has set us free. Stand firm, then, and do not let yourselves be burdened again by a yoke of slavery*' (Galatians 5:1). Very recently I saw a meme on social media that stated a very interesting fact. It read, 'Those who have the ability to forgive others tend to be happier and have longer life expectancy.' As you read this book, my prayer is that you will experience this true freedom, as well as a happier and longer life, as you experience the power in forgiveness.

Andrew Yelland, Pastor
Crofts End Church, Bristol

INTRODUCTION

For many Christians living the life as God instructs us to do in His Word is not always easy, especially if we don't stay close to the Lord. Over many years, I have had the joy of sharing the Word of God through testimony and preaching and there is nothing so joyful as seeing people's lives come to a fuller knowledge and understanding of God's Word.

However, there are times in our lives and Christian journey when we come up against trials that test our character and standing in Christ. Some of these tests and trials are the subject of unforgiveness and how we respond to dealing with such issues.

The origin of this book was borne out of a deep concern for the problems created by unforgiveness amongst those who claim to be Christians – having Jesus as Lord and Saviour. I too have been guilty of unforgiveness in my journey as a Christian, but came to the realisation of how important it is to read the Word of God and see the very clear instruction concerning this subject.

My place is not to judge people but to encourage them to read the scripture and see how relevant it is to their lives today and encourage them to live according to the Word.

This book I hope will be helpful, but let's be abundantly clear: it is no substitute for the written Word of God – the Bible.

My prayer is that you will be encouraged, released and set free if you have been or are struggling in the area of unforgiveness. If you know Jesus as Lord and Saviour then you will know He is able to carry us through any problems and difficulties of life if we allow Him in.

I have quoted a number of scriptures in this book; let me encourage you to look them up and read on for your benefit and further instruction from the Word of God.

CHAPTER ONE

POWER BELONGS TO GOD

It may come as no surprise to imagine the title of this chapter would be disputed by many world leaders who think that mankind can only rely on them and their politics to guide us through this life with meaning and purpose.

In reality, their ability to look much beyond their own circumstances without recourse to a higher authority is often revealed when problems arise. Being in a powerful position does not necessarily mean you are powerful. There will always be a limit to the power man can wield before the fallout comes.

The Bible says that power belongs to God (Psalm 62:11) among many other attributes that also belong to Him. He is not only the source of power but power began with Him. He is the Almighty God, creator of heaven and earth.

In Jeremiah 10:11 we read, '*These gods, who did not make the heavens and earth, will perish from the earth and from under the heavens.*' There are those down through history that have acquired so much power they themselves believed they were equal to God. '*The kings of the earth prepare for battle; the rulers plot together against the* Lord *and against his anointed one*' (Psalm 2:2 NLT).

'*He hath made the earth by his power, he hath established the world by his wisdom, and hath stretched out the heaven by his understanding*' (Jeremiah 51:15 KJV).

God's original intention for mankind is that he would embrace the heart of God through the demonstration of loving kindness, judgement and righteousness, all of which are found in Jesus. God's design for mankind was to have a relationship that would be everlasting. Man, however, when given a choice from the beginning of time made a decision that would rebound down through the ages, causing a serious breakdown in the relationship with a holy God.

In Psalm 62:12, David acknowledges that this all-powerful God is also a God of mercy which implies that judgement is necessary to deal with situations concerning the state of man and his conduct according to the Laws set out by God. It also means that man will now be judged according to our work or by how we live our lives and by our actions (v. 11). Here we are dealing with an Almighty God and a Merciful God, one who shows compassion, who gives confidence that we will be judged righteously by God who sees our every deed from afar off. In 1 Corinthians 3:8 we read, '*Each one will receive his own reward according to his own labour*' (NKJV). How did this all come about?

God's plan for man

Unless mankind is prepared to see himself as he is before Almighty God then the blindness of understanding could bring fatal consequences in the matter of eternity. The relationship between man and God was broken when sin came in the Garden of Eden. Sin means separation, isolation and no way back. The Bible is clear about sin, the consequences of which means eternal separation from God. He can neither be part of sin or look upon sin. Something had to happen to reconcile man back to God. God's plan was that we would have fellowship with Him for eternity, realising what He had done for us in creation that we may worship Him for who He is and in all the glory of His mighty works. Knowing God and knowing about God are two different things: the former speaks of something more intimate, something much closer, something that puts us in relationship with Him. For this to happen it means something radical has to change in our lives; if we have not already submitted to the will of God then now is the time to put right what is wrong. Don't let submission in this instance be seen as defeat; it is in fact stepping up to reality, realising our state before God and being prepared to do something about it. Unless we embrace God's plan for us all what future do we have? Remember the Bible says we will be judged by our works (actions). Becoming part of God's plan is a positive action on our behalf.

One of the biggest blockages to hearing the truth about God's plan for our lives is often related to excuse after excuse. Some will say I don't consider myself to be a bad person or a sinner, some would say I'm as good as the next person so why should I even think about being unacceptable to God? I can manage my own life, thanks, without any help from anybody else. All of these statements start with 'I' and unless 'I' is prepared to be given up or surrendered to God then the future is bleak! God is interested in you now – not yesterday or tomorrow but NOW! He wants to put right what is wrong and what will have lasting consequences for your life if you don't heed His Word (the Bible). God reminds us in scripture that 'all have sinned' and fallen short of God's standards for our lives. The nature of man is diametrically opposed to God's standards because the nature of man does wicked things and thinks evil thoughts, rejecting what God provided us with, which was a way back to Him by the cross of Jesus Christ His Son.

There's an old song that says:

There's a way back to God from the dark paths of sin;
There's a door that is open and all may go in:
At Calvary's cross is where you begin,
When you come as a sinner to Jesus.

We have very little excuse when we see that God who loves us so much sent His Son, the Lord Jesus, to die in our place, to cover our sin so that we would be acceptable to Him. The Bible says that the wages of sin is death; that means eternal separation from God. The only way we could be made right with God is through the righteousness of a perfect man in the Lord Jesus Christ. This means God had a plan to reconcile man back to Himself so that we might know His eternal plan for us.

Things eternal

How many of us invest in this life as though there is nothing beyond our current existence? Too often we feel we must have the latest thing, particularly where technology is concerned, in case we are out of touch or don't know what's going on around us. Somehow this could speak of insecurities in some folks' lives, they just can't imagine not being in the know or seeming to be uninformed. There is a saying that we came into the world with nothing and we will leave it with nothing. Not even the ancient pharaohs could take their gold and precious belongings beyond the grave. So why is it we cling to things that over time can depreciate in value and use? Our lives can become cluttered with items that do no more than collect dust and in some cases fade away no matter how they might have once been treasured.

The moment we cling to what we think is ours is the moment we could be asked how willing are we to give it up. In Matthew 19 we read the account of the rich young ruler who wanted to know how to get eternal life. Jesus then says something interesting: *'If you want to be perfect, go, sell your possessions and give to the poor, and you will have treasure in heaven. Then come follow me'* (v. 21).

What was going on here is that Jesus was challenging the man to see how much he loved what he had. This young man went away sad because he had many riches which were more important than anything else.

Some of us can identify with this young man, especially if we have allowed our possessions to become more important than loving God. You might not consider any of your possessions more important than God but consider this: would you sell or give away your most prized possession, the very thing that you would say means the world to you?

When God handed down the Ten Commandments to Moses the very first commandment said, *'You shall have no other gods before me'* (Exodus 20:2). To enjoy the fullness of God's blessing He commands that we should put away any distraction other than total commitment to Him. God's plan for us is to make us into the kind of people that will one day share eternity with Him. Just like children, we need to be shown the right way going forward even if it means being chastised along the way.

When the apostle Paul writes to the church at Colossae he reminds them to set their minds on the things above (Colossians 3:1). Why? Because Paul wanted the church to remember that they had committed their lives to Christ and that their 'affections' were in another direction, not to concentrate on the things of earth which are corruptible and will one day disappear.

Ephesians 3 speaks of the eternal purpose of God through Christ. Have you ever imagined that we who have accepted Jesus as our Saviour are called to much higher purposes even whilst we are still on earth? God has blessed us with every spiritual blessing (Ephesians 1:3); God has chosen us to be holy (Ephesians 1:4); God has adopted us and made us acceptable in Christ (Ephesians 1:5-6); God has redeemed us by the blood of Jesus so that our sins are forgiven and we are now made acceptable to a holy God (Ephesians 1:7). What has been promised by the Father is made possible through the Son Jesus and is confirmed by the Holy Spirit who is there to guide us into all truth. These are eternal things that begin now and last for all eternity.

There is no doubt that life is all about choices, some we make can be good choices and for our benefit, but some are not so good and to our detriment; we find out by the consequences of bad decisions. A very interesting television documentary programme has in its introduction words like 'Life as we know it'. It suggests that life as portrayed in the film is all there is and nothing outside of it. How can we experience life, but in hindsight, God is offering another opportunity for all.

Jesus said He has come that we might have life and eternal life at that (John 10:10). So why is it so difficult to make decisions that are for our good? Is it because we only see the now? Or just a short time ahead because we are unable to comprehend anything beyond this? Is it maybe because we are so indoctrinated by outside influences that seem more plausible? Whatever takes control of your life may dictate your destiny unless you are ready to step outside your comfort zone. To think of 'things eternal' for many will be too much to take on board.

When a young eagle wants to learn to fly it watches its parents spread their wings and mimic the actions of flight. Until the young eagles begin to spread their wings they are going nowhere fast. In simple terms: actions produce results. This applies to the actions needed when seeking to make the right decisions that could affect the rest of your days. Making a change for the good as a result of the action you take could have much wider consequences that are far more reaching than you can possibly imagine. As you travel through this life you will undoubtedly make some mistakes but you don't have to be defeated by those mistakes if you are willing to learn from them.

A few years ago I spent some time ministering in prisons, taking the good news of Jesus to those who had made wrong decisions. Many I spoke to said the reason they were behind bars was due to listening to voices in their heads. They said that they didn't want to do the things that they did but felt the voice was so real it pushed them into committing the crime that influenced their lives and resulted in incarceration.

Jesus said, '*I have come to set the captive free*' (Luke 4:18). What He is talking about is that we can be free from sin and the influence of any other voice outside of His.

That also means we can begin to understand the importance of things eternal, things that will influence our lives for the good, leading us to live the life God intended for us until we reign with Him.

In contrast to things eternal, the Bible refers to the works of the old nature which deserves death and cause death because of sin. One of those works is double-mindedness. Jesus says we can't serve two masters (Matthew 6:24). If we are opening our minds to any unknown voices then how can we know if what we hear is good for us? In John 10 Jesus speaks of the Parable of the Good Shepherd and He makes a point that the sheep (His followers – you and me) not only hear His voice but obey His voice. Later on in these verses Jesus also says He is the Good Shepherd who gives life to His followers. What Jesus wants us to understand is that our lives are safe with Him. He won't ask us or lead us to do things that cause death and destruction.

The plan in place

Things eternal are things that last for ever, so what we do now will impact our lives for the future, making the right decision at the right time, not listening to false voices or being influenced by things around us that have a minus value and can lead to destruction.

Time and time again you will see advertisements or television adverts promoting the value of having a will generally appealing to the older generation. As most will know, this is to set out what you wish to leave for loved ones or relatives and maybe organisations you feel particularly supportive of, when you leave this life. It generally sets out what items of value or interest you think will be appreciated by those who succeed you. Sadly, a will can be the source of great debate and even argument amongst those who survive and are either mentioned in the will or not! Families have fallen apart over such things. However, the detail in the will is the desire of the one who has passed on. Inheritance is not always a blessing, especially when our forebears have not considered the consequences of their requests. Thankfully this is not the case when it comes to heaven. God in His wisdom has promised His plan is not only perfect but will accomplish all beyond our imagination and to His glory.

God's plan – a plan of salvation – is that none should perish. However, not all will see the Lord. Salvation is deliverance from destruction and judgement and death. And it is the choice open to everyone by putting their trust in Jesus Christ as their Saviour and Lord. This is the tremendous provision of the Father through the Son.

This is the will of God in salvation that none should perish; there is salvation from sin (Romans 10:10); salvation from physical infirmity (Acts 4:10,12); salvation from death and destruction (Romans 13:11). Just think, salvation is mentioned over 100 times in scripture and is translated as meaning deliverance, save, health, help, victory and rescue to name a few. Now, if that isn't a plan . . . !

In an earthly sense a will can have a counter-productive benefit to those who inherit, simply because of the problems – although not intended – it can create when there are others in the family who believe they should have benefited in some way or another but for some reason have been left out completely. This causes conflict and allows Satan to creep in and stir up even more of a mess. If there is one thing

Satan tries to do it is to cause disharmony and strife in family life.

The wonderful thing about God for us is that He is all inclusive; no one who has accepted Jesus as Lord and Saviour and who is destined for heaven is left out. That applies to the fact that we already begin to enjoy the benefits of God's will for our lives as we live in His Spirit daily (Romans 2:7).

In God's plan we are encouraged to walk in the newness of life Jesus has given us (Romans 6:4). Sometimes it's a tall order, yet the Holy Spirit is right here to help and guide us step by step, not only in direction but thought and deed. The plan is in place, it's whether we realise it's there for our good and life-long benefit. It affects our lives, how we live and how we grow as Christians.

Preparation time

As with all good plans the most successful are based on good preparation. Time when all the equipment is planned out and the strategy is put in place. So it is in the Christian life; if we are to be effective not only in our personal life but our ministry as well, we need to prepare well. I believe it was R.T. Kendall who said that all ministers of God should spend at least two hours a day in the Word of God. Why? How are you going to know and love and understand the one who you represent on earth unless you know Him through His Word. You may not think you have it in you to be useful for God; you may think my life has been such a disappointment to me, so how can God use me? Just look in 1 Corinthians 1:27 which says, 'But God has chosen the foolish things of the world to put to shame the wise; and God has chosen the *weak things of the world to put to shame the things which are mighty.*' Some folk have fallen into the trap of thinking that unless you are of some social standing or maybe you have acquired the achievements recognised by society or your financial status is such that you are not qualified to stand up for Jesus. Don't let this lie stay with you for one moment longer. It is not from God. Isn't it great God doesn't look on the outside to see the heart of man but deep inside to know the man of God? Sadly there are those who get all puffed up when position in their eyes elevates them to a higher station for all to see! This is not the person God is able to use in His plan. If we are to be used to glorify God then we need to learn from the supreme example of Jesus – we will be looking at this in the next chapter. Remember God didn't call us because we were wise or of great standing. He calls in spite of all that man may think of himself. It isn't what we have or what we have achieved in this world that guarantees eternal life. The message of the gospel is offensive because it puts to shame those who think that they are good enough for anything, even eternity. So part of our preparation is to appreciate that it's not according to our condition or position but our willingness to be humbled for the service of the Lord.

If we mean business with God and we really want to conquer some of the weaknesses in our lives then we must be prepared for battle! There is an enemy who will try to dissuade you from doing the right thing and robbing you of the life you can lead in Christ. So where do we start to prepare to step up to the plan that God wants for us as individuals? What we are wanting to do is to show people by example that it is not 'I' but Christ in me that is more important because without Christ we have nothing to offer that will impact and change another person's life. What the Bible encourages us to do is to ensure that our testimony is one where Christ is seen in me. For this to happen there may be issues that you are yet to deal with and we will address some of these later in this book.

The title of this book is *The Power in Forgiveness*. We need to meet the One who has the power to forgive and then we need to understand that this same power is available to us by way of being forgiven. Don't assume that because you have asked for forgiveness for things in the past, you don't need to seek further for forgiveness concerning other matters that may have not been dealt with or have happened since. Why is this so important? Because we are still earthly beings and subject to the things around us that can draw us away from God unless we keep a short account and stay close to Him. Satan is on the warpath and is out to trip us up and defeat us at every opportunity. You may not think a small lie or a swear word is necessarily a problem, but consider whether it honours God and represents His Word in our lives. It's sometimes the smallest things that can cause the biggest problems. So what am I trying to say? Let God work in your life in His way to show you how much you are worth in Him. I remember a story from my youth which has stuck with me – it goes like this. There was a little boy watching a great sculptor work with a block of marble. The young boy asks the sculptor what he is about to make. The sculptor replies, 'I'm about to make a lion.'

The boy responds, 'How are you going to make a lion out of a block of marble?'

'Ah!' the sculptor says. 'I'm going to chip away everything that isn't lion!'

Isn't this the way that God lovingly deals with us? Patiently He chips away everything that is either not good for us or is not part of His plan for us if we allow Him to. When we committed our lives to Christ we gave over our right to dictate how He should treat us. The Bible says He is a loving Father and only wants the best for His children. There are occasions when, just like children, we need to be taught things along the way, lessons that we may find hard to learn but all of which are in our interest. Just like the sculptor who could see the finished article before he started chipping away at the marble block, our Father in heaven sees the finished work in us through the cross of Calvary. Over the years I have heard people say what's the point of living? Well, unless you get to know the One who gave you life, you may never know.

When I started work as a trainee architect I had no idea where it would lead, but one thing was sure: as a young Christian I wanted to serve the Lord in my job. When I left school I had no idea I would get a job in an architect's office let alone have access to a profession that would carry me throughout my working life and beyond. God had already worked out the plan for my life a long time ago. What He wanted from me was surrender to His ideal for my life. I was fifteen, I didn't know at the time that He knew the desires of my heart. All the same, after ten to fifteen years of working with all sorts of building design and construction, the opportunity came for me to specialise in ecclesiastical building design. I spent the major part of my life in architecture and building surveying, specialising in church design and construction. Little did I realise those early years of my working life were all preparation for the main event!

God hasn't given up on you. Maybe if He's got your attention then He can begin chipping away all that is not really you, so that the real person in Christ can be seen.

CHAPTER TWO

NO OTHER SACRIFICE

Modern society is governed by the law and today we rely on the law to keep us safe from those who wish to flout or openly disregard the law. The Bible tells us that man by nature is sinful and that suggests it's more likely that we are drawn to do the things that will either disobey the law or out rightly reject the law.

From the beginning of time when God gave man a choice to either obey His instruction or to go a separate way, the wrong choice was made and the world now pays for the consequences of a bad decision! The decision not to obey God was through disobedience. The problem here was Adam and Eve couldn't see beyond their action and all that it might bring. This is an example of sin where we don't think it's wrong to take an action in our own strength, even if it's against God, yet we will bear the consequences. Even though we have the benefit of a higher authority to help us and guide us through life, if we choose to go our own way then we are responsible for the outcome. In Genesis 2 you can read the account of God's plan to have a relationship with mankind, to give man responsibility and duties to share in looking after creation, even to have a companion in Eve as a wife. God's intention was for the good of mankind. But because Eve decided to listen to another voice and draw Adam into the action that would change the course for mankind, sin entered in and the fall of man has since rebounded down through the ages. Because of this, not only was a close relationship with God broken but the result of sin is death. God's intention was that His plan was for eternity and originally it included man, but now the plan had to be changed! The whole approach to God had to be restructured, the directness that could have been enjoyed by Adam and Eve was lost so another way had to come into being. God in His nature and love for the world was not prepared to give up on man but to continue to demonstrate His amazing love and compassion for us.

In the Old Testament the people were governed by the Law. The Law was aligned to the sin of not measuring up to the covenants made in that day. The Bible says that '*without the shedding of blood there is no remission [for sin]*' (Hebrews 9:22 NKJV). A structure was put in place for the priests of the temple to receive animal sacrifices so that blood could be shed for the sins of the people. The priests' job was to bring the blood offering to the Lord, making atonement for the people. The word 'atonement' has several meanings: it's to cleanse, cancel, appease and purge, to name a few. Nonetheless, it also meant 'sacrifice' – an act of giving up something valued for the sake of something else regarded as more important or worthy. Well, that's the dictionary's definition anyway. But there are key words here: 'the act of giving up'. I would put more of a slant on it by saying 'something that is going to cost' or 'letting go of something that you regarded as yours'! Reaching the mark of permanent cleansing and forgiveness could not be accomplished by the Law; this was only made possible by

Jesus at the cross of Calvary. The Law was unable to free people from sin and death, it was unable to justify and redeem the sinner to God. It was also unable to prevent man from sinning further. No wonder something more profound had to happen; what real hope did man have other than a perfect sacrifice that would please God on all fronts? Something had to happen that was going to last forever if there was a way back to God. That means a sacrifice which would bring complete atonement and reconciliation; it would mean we need a high priest who lives forever to intercede on our behalf before a holy God. There had to be one who could fulfil this weighty role and who would be able to stand before our maker. The world needed a Saviour then and needs a Saviour today.

Jesus the supreme example

Amongst the famous hymns written by Cecil Frances Alexander (1818–1895), who was an Anglo-Irish hymn writer and poet, was the hymn 'There Is a Green Hill Far Away'. She also wrote 'All Things Bright and Beautiful' and the Christmas carol 'Once in Royal David's City'. In the hymn 'There is a Green Hill Far Away' are some words that in short sum up what I want to say:

> There was no other good enough
> To pay the price of sin;
> He only could unlock the gate
> Of heav'n, and let us in.

For a holy God there had to be a perfect sacrifice. Hebrews 10:1 says, '*For the law . . . can never with these same sacrifices, which they offer continually year by year, make those who approach perfect*' (NKJV). If this were the case then the people would have continued with sacrifices as being sufficient. In verse 3, *'But in those sacrifices there is a reminder of sins every year'* (NKJV). Something had to be done that would deal with sin once and for all. Jesus came in the flesh to do His Father's will, to be *'obedient unto death'* (Philippians 2:8 KJV). Jesus came that the old system could be abolished and a new covenant established. Remember what the verse in the hymn says: 'There was no other good enough to pay the price of sin.' Only Jesus, the perfect, spotless Lamb of God, could replace the old Law. Believers in Christ have now been sanctified by Christ's death on the cross; the old Law could not do this. The purification of worshippers under the Law had to be repeatedly conducted day after day, year after year. The reason Jesus was the supreme example of the sacrifice acceptable to God, is that He was the spotless, perfect 'Lamb', blameless, pure and holy. Christ's sacrifice was once and for all, never to be repeated. The Bible says that after Jesus ascended to heaven He sat down at the right hand of the Father, His work completed. What thousands of sacrifices under the old system could not do, Jesus accomplished at Calvary.

Perhaps not always fully appreciated is that because of the sacrifice Jesus made at Calvary we have access to God. The Bible tells us that in the tabernacle the inner-most place was called the Holy of Holies, a place where the priests were only allowed to enter once a year. To separate this area of the tabernacle was a thick veil; it was the barrier between the people and God. When Jesus died on the cross this veil that separated the people from God was torn in two, giving full access to all. Jesus opened a way to God. Now we can boldly approach the throne (Hebrews 4:16); it's through the blood of Jesus, the perfect sacrifice, that we can approach the throne of grace. Go back to Hebrews 7:25 and you will read, '*He is also able to save to the uttermost those who come to God through Him, since He always lives to make intercession for them*' (NKJV). What a fantastic thought that no longer do I have to wonder if my sins will separate me from God for eternity. All because Jesus is standing there before the throne of grace saying to the Father that I am worthy to be called a child of God. Let's make no mistake, if we are to approach God, we need to understand that we too have obligations. Because God is light, we too are expected to walk in the light. '*If we walk in the light as he is in the light, we have fellowship with one another, and the blood of Jesus Christ, his Son, purifies us from all sin*' (1 John 1:7). If we know there is sin in us how much better is it to confess that sin? In this same chapter is the wonderful reminder, 'He is faithful and just to forgive us our sins and purify us from all unrighteousness' (v. 9). A good friend of mine said many years ago, 'When considering our sinful state before a most holy God it is best to keep a short account,' simply meaning, if we know we have sinned then take it to the Lord who is able to forgive our sin and remember them no more. There are no sizes or grades to sin – just SIN – the barrier between God and man. If we are to grow in Christ, then we need to follow His example and obey His Word in our lives. If the Christian sets his or her life in the hope of the Christ of Calvary and trusts on the promise of the Word of God then their lives will be steadfast in Him.

For all mankind to see

When Jesus walked this earth His ministry was very public; more so was His crucifixion. Man has little excuse to say he did not know. The Bible, the best- and longest-selling book of all time, has probably reached most nations and peoples on this earth and still there seems to be a lack of understanding of the treasures therein. We know there is another force trying to defeat the power of the Word of God getting out and into the lives of people in this world. The reason Satan does not want to let this happen is simply because Satan does not want you to know the truth about him or what future he doesn't have; he is only interested in keeping you away from God and robbing you of your freedom in Jesus Christ. Satan is the prince of darkness and that's where he wants you to stay – in the dark.

Jesus reminds us in John 3:19-20 that *'men loved darkness rather than light, because their deeds were evil. For everyone practising evil hates the light and does not come to the light, lest his deeds should be exposed'* (NKJV). When Jesus, the Light of the World, comes in to our lives He not only exposes those things that hold us back and hinder us from growing in Him but bind us from the freedom we can know in Him.

Remember He has come to set the captive free. Men in darkness can only perform those things of darkness, but thanks to the work of Christ there is another way and mankind would be better served to not only realise this but to take advantage of the offer of freedom in Christ.

John 3:16, one of the most beautiful verses in scripture in my opinion, is that God loved the world so much that He was prepared to sacrifice His Son, the Lord Jesus, to bare the sins of you and me, so that we no longer are condemned to eternal damnation and separation from God. His intention from the beginning of time is that we should not perish but have communion with Him for eternity. He loves us that much. Jesus made a very public statement when hanging on the cross at Calvary. He was there in our place, He bore our sin and shame, He was saying loud and clear that God loves the world and wants fellowship with us.

If your experience of God has cooled and you may have drifted away – possibly because of disappointment, rejection or doubt – and this has caused a loss of belonging, you feel no interest in reading the Word or praying, everything seems less important . . . you need to know that God hasn't moved away from you. It is so easy to bail out of something that doesn't give you what you want when you want it. Imagine what would have happened if Jesus said to the Father in heaven, 'I don't want to go to the cross, I don't want to die' – where would we be today? If you committed your life to Christ it is no longer yours, you gave it over to the Saviour who paid a great price for you and loves you with an everlasting love. This is a love that will never let you go. For most this would be real assurance that there is a purpose for our salvation in Jesus. Jesus was obedient even unto death on the cross, the Bible tells us; what better example of fulfilling the Father's plan to win us all back to Him. God didn't wait for us to call Him; He came to seek out the lost. He knew we needed Him as much as He longs for us to know how much He loves us and wants to show what He has in store for us beyond this life. Ask yourself this question: is it not sufficient that our names are recorded in the Lamb's Book of Life when we give our lives to Jesus? Do you see what we did the moment we asked Christ into our lives was to get our citizenship to heaven, a life beyond this life, for all eternity (Philippians 4:3)? It's all because of Jesus that we have the right to enter heaven. If you feel a failure, join the queue! There are many Christians who have come up against this trial before. Remember failure does not have to be final. Maybe you need to stand still, take stock and reconsider your position? Disappointment need not rob you of being happy and fulfilled.

Rejection need not rob you of acceptance.

Doubt need not rob you of conviction and confidence.

Christ came that we might have life and life more abundantly, not something short of all He has to bless us.

Perhaps one of the most profound things in scripture is when the veil in the temple was torn in two. This signified the end of the Old Testament religion. No longer did the people have to wait till the priest would go into the Holy of Holies because access to God was now direct through Jesus Christ. The accomplished work of Calvary was announced by Jesus crying out, '*It is finished*' (John 19:30). This ended the religious system once and for all. Everything that was set up as part of the religious system was no longer relevant or required; the perfect sacrifice had been made. Most importantly here was the fact that the whole purpose of the cross was for the whole world, Jew and Gentile alike. Furthermore, Jesus had broken the power of sin over mankind. No longer was death so final. No longer would the power of sin have such a hold on man that there was no other escape. In Romans 7 we read the limitations of the Law, but since the cross there is a way back to God. Satan wants the believers to think that for once you have sinned there is no way out of it; you will have to live with your sin for the rest of your life. If this were true then Calvary was a waste of time! But we know otherwise, because Jesus accomplished victory over death and sin at Calvary. Because death no longer had dominion over Christ (Romans 6:9-14) because Jesus rose again, so shall we who put our trust in Him. Romans 8 is such a powerful chapter in scripture, so releasing when you realise what and who we are in Christ. When we wake up to the truth of these words then we will begin to realise the power in forgiveness. Be sure to understand the obligation on our part: we are expected to walk in the light of Christ not to live by our old nature before we met Jesus as Lord and Saviour. Go back to chapter 6 in Romans and you will see what Paul is saying to the believers in Rome. You don't have to continue in your old ways – that was not fruitful in your life – so put those things out of your life and live as Christ would have you live. How wonderful to think we are under the continuous grace and mercy of God every day of our lives when we put our trust in Him.

A legacy for now!

Normally we consider a legacy to be something someone leaves to another in a will, something you may benefit from or perhaps is your birth right. This is a little more personal to you. What sort of legacy will you leave when you finally depart this earth? All that you have read up until now is the everlasting legacy from heaven. Jesus made promises that He knew would be kept for time immemorial; they weren't loose promises but those that would have a profound effect on you and me. When Jesus ascended to heaven that was not to leave us wondering what was next; He had already explained to the disciples and followers that He would come again to meet His bride (the church) to join Him for eternity. What you leave will be something for now. But this could be dramatically changed to something that could be a lifeline to another person. You may think you have very little to pass on to anyone, but if you have put your trust in the Lord you are rich beyond belief, because what you have to give is more far reaching than something that will only last for a while. One of the greatest privileges we have as believers is to pass on the message of the gospel of Jesus Christ; it is the most valuable thing we can give to another. You may wish to leave earthly mementos to your loved ones as they will without doubt have sentimental or even monetary value, but nothing will compare with passing on a legacy that will have eternal value. Now, we don't have the privilege as the disciples of old who walked and talked with Jesus in person, yet we have just the same privilege of being guided and led by the Holy Spirit. Part of what Christ was saying before He ascended to heaven was, 'I will not leave you without help or comfort.' In fact He said, 'I must go so the Comforter may come' (see John 16:7). This was now the Holy Spirit's time to help and guide us to the truth and empower us to do the work of God. That work includes spreading the good news of Jesus Christ. The beginning of the 'everlasting legacy' is the moment you surrender your life to Christ. The Holy Spirit is there to confirm your new relationship with God through Jesus.

What you have probably appreciated by now is that Jesus never made a promise He couldn't keep. Sadly, we, on the other hand, are not able to sustain this position in life as many of us fail in this department! The amazing thing is this: we are not asked to keep the promise of what God has provided for His children; we are only asked to point people in the right direction. That is the cross of Calvary. The promise that has been made for each individual is a personal gift from God through His Son to everyone who believes in Him. Isn't it interesting to note that unless we feel we have all the latest gizmos to impress the church with today we can't do our work effectively? Let me take you into the early chapters of Acts. What do you see? Did the disciples have the latest all-singing-all-dancing IT equipment to set up before they could preach the gospel? Of course not! But what they did have was more important and more effective than all the gear in the world put together and that was the power of the Holy Spirit in their lives. Of course, I'm not knocking the advancement of technology or the benefits it brings to our church environment, but it is no substitute for the power of God's Spirit working through us. Whatever we do for God is not by our own strength. Zechariah 4:6 reminds us that it's God's power that makes things possible. Remember when we share Christ to another person it's not us doing the witnessing but Christ witnessing through us! So, where does that put us in this situation concerning a legacy? What we have to give is usually of material value; what we have to give in Christ is of eternal value. So the great commission still stands for the church today: we have the joy of sharing what Jesus did for us and that this gift of eternal life in Him is still available to all. Let it be said that what you left behind was priceless and for all eternity. Jesus by example shows us 'a better way' – it's our obligation to pass this on. A legacy for now has an end date. The legacy from heaven is forever!

CHAPTER THREE

WHO IS ONESIMUS?

Some of the more obscure characters in the Bible can have an impact in the way we approach things in this life. Onesimus has always interested me simply because he was to the society of his day someone who had little position; in fact he was a slave. Yet as we will explore, he played a particular role by which his experience can teach us a few things. It should be said that Onesimus came into contact with people who also influenced his future. Wouldn't it be interesting if we knew early on in our journey through life that the people we meet may have a real impact on the way our life pans out? Arguably, not all people we meet will be a blessing to us and at worst may take us down the wrong road.

So, what was it about this man that is so interesting? Sometimes in scripture we read about great men and women who have been recognised by their actions and most were not in the same category as Onesimus. What brought Onesimus to my attention was the fact that although a slave he seemed to be not unlike some of us. He was prepared to break free from his commitment to his master for reason to travel, whether this was to escape his bond to his master Philemon or something else, we may not know the full story. However, Onesimus had travelled some distance when he came across a man named Paul. Now the problem was Paul was in Rome in prison yet this encounter changed the future for Onesimus. Sometimes situations can take us way out of familiar surroundings for us to encounter unexpected events and circumstances, for Onesimus this was one of those occasions. The reason Onesimus was on the run was because he had robbed his master; he knew if he was to get away he would need money that he did not have, so he decided to take some from his master and run. Approximately 1500 kilometres later he arrived in Rome and amazingly had a meeting with Paul the apostle. I doubt this was on his agenda when he set out from Colossae in Asia Minor. But this was going to change his life and direction.

Onesimus was a runaway, he had something to hide and thought that going far away from the problem would vindicate him and ease his conscience. What is interesting about this is that Onesimus made it to Rome and probably thought he would not be known to anyone and be lost in the crowds of the city and that would be sweet relief to his conscience. Yet it appears he needed a friend, somebody to help him. It's possible he ran out of money or he needed somewhere to stay. Perhaps he remembered his master talking about this man called Paul who was in prison in Rome and decided to look him up! It's reasonable to think that Paul was his only hope – Onesimus had no friends in Rome that we know of, yet Paul was a name he knew and decided to see if Paul could help him. How many times do we have to learn that running away from a problem does not solve it? It may go away for a period of time but it will always be there lurking at the back of our mind. The restless mind at night that robs so many of sleep and the troubled mind in the day frustrates your work or social pattern, all of which means we are carrying loads that we don't have to. It doesn't matter how far you run, your conscience goes with you!

Friend of a friend

Onesimus probably didn't think it that important to have to go back and put anything right with Philemon, but unless something happened he was going to be carrying a burden for a very long time. While Onesimus was serving Philemon it's more than likely he heard of Paul as they were brothers in Christ and friends. It was possibly this friendship that had a purpose in the situation Onesimus finds himself now. Exactly what the introduction was like when Onesimus walked into the prison to see Paul we don't know, but I'm sure Paul, even if he didn't recognise Onesimus, would have been gracious enough to receive him. Whatever happened, Paul found Onesimus to be a great helper to him, which suggests time passed by as they got to know each other.

I believe Paul found not only a friend in Onesimus but someone who could assist him in his work. Paul at this time was able to lead Onesimus to Christ (Philemon 10). This is it, the life-changing moment for Onesimus, something that was going to deal with the burden he was carrying. So, Paul does the right thing. Normally when Paul would write to Philemon, a man named Tychicus would be the bearer of the letters to the church – in this case Paul tells Onesimus that he must return to his master and that Tychicus will go with him. Whether that made Onesimus feel any better about going back to his master we don't know. Normally if slaves ran away from their masters the punishment would be very harsh and could even mean death. The difference this time is that Onesimus, whilst with Paul, became a Christian and Paul wants to make it clear to Philemon that his servant is now also a brother in Christ (v. 16). So Paul being a friend of a friend became a new friend to the runaway slave. In Philemon verse 12 Paul says, '*I am sending him back. You therefore receive him, that is, my own heart.*' Paul was confident in Philemon that he would dispense justice wisely.

Just another slave

Philemon could have treated Onesimus as just another slave and punished him even to the point of expelling him from his home and service. After all, it's possible Philemon had other slaves and, even if not, he would know there were plenty out there in the markets to buy. But all of a sudden something changed the whole character of this slave. No longer was Onesimus just an ordinary slave; he was a born-again slave with a future. Part of his future was to character build in him the new life that he had committed to in Christ. First, he was going to have to humble himself before his master and seek forgiveness for what he had done. It may be that Onesimus brought embarrassment and shame on his master for what he did, it may have been stealing the money completely destroyed the trust that his master wanted to have in him. Whatever it was, it needed to be put right for the relationship between Onesimus and Philemon to be restored.

The damage that was caused by Onesimus could have been unrepairable with no going back. That would have certainly put Onesimus in a predicament. Just like us if we allow a wrong to go on without addressing it, it is not only a sin accounted against us, it dishonours God. As much as Paul would have liked Philemon to agree to let Onesimus stay in Rome with him he realises the importance of putting a wrong right. You might say what difference would it make to Onesimus who was a slave and always would be a slave? Well, he certainly didn't have to be a slave to sin, and then he also didn't have to live a life without purpose by doing the right thing and returning to his master. He certainly won't know how he would be received until he got back to Philemon. This time he had a reference, something that would certainly not be common to all slaves! This was not just any reference, it was a character reference from a highly respected man of God. An endorsement that would have meant a lot in the day. Not only did he have a reference but he had a promise for his debt to be paid in full. Until a wrong is put right then it is still an outstanding debt and unless this is settled, we are carrying the burden until we are released from it. Jesus paid the debt of us all at the cross so we might be free of any liability to any man, even to God for the sins we have committed. Surely it is our part to play and ensure we are not debtors so that we don't dishonour the one who did it all for us. In simple language, there was a time when Paul states Onesimus was considered useless to Philemon but has now become useful to both him and Philemon. Times have changed for Onesimus; whilst on one occasion he is considered useless he has now the term 'useful' being identified with his character! The change would be evident in the matter and conduct that Onesimus would display when back in the presence of his master. Just think, this somewhat dejected man, until he heard the good news of Jesus Christ was on a no-hope course to possible destruction. But when God enters in, the pathway was made straight, straight to the person that would be instrumental in Onesimus' conversion.

Promotion in love

I wonder what your initial reaction would have been to Onesimus if you were in Philemon's shoes? Did Philemon need Onesimus? Probably not as much as Onesimus needed Philemon. Here was a master who was to all intents and purposes rich enough to go and buy another slave, but this was not how the story went. Something happened that changed the whole situation; something, some would say, not natural! It's easy at this stage to focus on Onesimus simply because he was the person in the wrong and yet it was not by chance that the circumstances were to change the outcome of this episode of Onesimus' life. It would have been perfectly normal by human reaction for Philemon to feel let down, disappointed in Onesimus as he was given a home and a job. Doubtless Philemon would have also been hurt by the course that Onesimus decided to embark on, especially as he had to break the law in doing so. We don't really know what was behind Onesimus' thinking when he decided to rob his master and flee. It would not be unreasonable to think that Onesimus should have been punished for his wrong, but this was not to be. From afar off God saw the situation and God had His man in place, albeit a prison, and this was to change the whole outcome of Onesimus' wrongdoing.

However Onesimus found Paul we don't know, but he did and through it he became a Christian just like his master.

Not only did this have an impact on his life but his conscience; it's likely Onesimus underwent a crash course in the fundamentals of the Christian life under Paul's teaching. He doubtless would have been taught about the love of Christ and how he forgives us our sins and paid an incredible price to win us back to Him. He would have been taught the importance of honesty and openness if he wanted true friendship and fellowship; he would have been taught that his whole life was now given over to the Saviour Jesus Christ and that he was now to live as an example of what Christ had done for him. It's possible Onesimus may have seen some of these examples in his master's life and didn't at the time realise that this was going to become part of him in the future.

The return from Rome must have felt like a journey half-way around the world for Onesimus, his mind rehearsing what he would say and do when he got home, even though he had Paul's letter of reference. Saying sorry is not always an easy thing especially if it is meant from the heart and in true repentance of the wrong. What sort of reception was waiting for him? This is not quite the Prodigal Son's story, yet there is a similarity. Even though the father in the case of the prodigal son's account saw him afar off and ran to meet him, this time the circumstances were slightly different. The one thing in common with both accounts is that the masters of each of the homes were examples of men whose lives were changed because of love in their hearts. I believe when Paul wrote to Philemon he wrote because he knew they firstly had a common bond in love through Christ. The singer Michael Ball recorded a song some years ago called 'Love Changes Everything' and in this account, that was about to happen. Not only did Paul appeal to Philemon to demonstrate love through forgiveness, he wanted him to reinstate his slave even though he had been wronged. Paul must have found it hard to let Onesimus go as he had benefited from having a pair of hands and feet to help him in his present predicament. Onesimus paradoxically had freedom that Paul did not have, and yet Paul knew he had to send Onesimus back to Philemon as this was the right and correct thing to do, especially as something had to take place for forgiveness and healing to bear fruit. What Paul was getting across to Philemon is that even though he had been robbed, the slave was not the same; now he was a new man something had changed and put him on an equal footing in Christ. Onesimus could have been completely written off from being useless to being completely rejected and cast out, maybe what he deserved, but the love of Christ did change everything. Jesus said, 'If we let sin take over then we will be slaves to sin' (John 8:34 paraphrased).

There's no account how Philemon received Onesimus, but there is a confident account of how Paul saw events unfolding based on his knowledge of a friend who could and would love like Christ because of the change in his life. Paul knew his friend Philemon and shared a love that only comes from God. It's a love that will not let you down but one you can rely on even when you are apart and at a distance. I like to think that although the very first moments of this reconciliation might have been slightly difficult, this would also have been short lived because of the power in forgiveness. I like to think that Philemon would have received Onesimus as Paul expected of him and as Paul says in Philemon 21, I'm sure you will go further than just to reinstate our now brother in the Lord. What a transformation from robber to brother, from slave to someone with identity in Jesus Christ. Sometimes we wonder how on earth did that happen? Promoted in love through being brought to the Lord by a man in prison, to being forgiven by a master who should have cast him out. Facing up to our wrongs is not expected to be easy but when we are free of our wrongdoing then our burden is light! When you find yourself in a dark place because of something you have done wrong or you know should be put right, then ask God to help you put it right. Onesimus not only became a brother, but a son in the spiritual sense and an heir to the throne of grace. We are completely changed when Jesus is invited in to make the difference. Being loved and accepted is transformational.

CHAPTER FOUR

BY EXAMPLE

The apostle Paul

One of the great Bible stories of old is the conversion of Saul of Tarsus; if you know your Bible then you will know the story. There are, however, plenty of lessons to be learnt from the account that happened to Saul and the immediate events that followed. To remind ourselves, Saul was a highly educated man, and he was on a mission which he believed was in support of the Jewish traditions of the day. Saul didn't believe in Jesus being the Messiah. He was unable to see the purpose of the cross other than a place of punishment for criminals; it was a place of finality no coming back!

At this time Saul considered his mission as one of justification based on the fact that any Jews who we're purporting that Jesus was alive and is the Messiah were agents of Satan and were heretics, the type of people that needed to be stamped out due to the contradiction of that being preached by the Pharisees. So, Saul goes to the high priests and gets authority to bring Christians believing that Jesus is the Messiah back to Jerusalem for trial. What Saul wasn't expecting was the events that would happen on his way to Damascus. He was about to become the centre of the biggest roadside experience ever recorded. Talk about a 'breakdown', this was to become the biggest fall down! It must have been quite a fall; I don't know how many hands Saul's horse was high but he would have known by how hard he hit the ground. Sometimes when God wants to get our attention, we to have to hit the ground to realise we need to stop and take a moment to listen. Saul didn't just fall off his horse – he was far too experienced a horseman for this to happen – but here he was. Even before he could wipe the dust off himself, he heard a voice calling him from heaven by name. Immediately Saul enquires, 'Who are you, Lord?' Here is the moment of revelation because the answer came, *'I am Jesus, whom you are persecuting'* (Acts 9:5). Even Saul's escort were bowed down not understanding the conversation that was taking place. Eventually, they all get up and Saul is on a detour.

Saul's whole world was about to change: he started the day on a journey of spiritual blindness, then he became blind for a period of three days before his eyes were opened not just physically but spiritually as he was shown things he would never have seen in his former state.

Saul was about to be shaken at the very core of his own understanding; as a Pharisee he would have to climb down and humble himself to repent of his sins. His encounter with Jesus was so exposing, it would have revealed not only the truth but the condition of the person before a holy God. Just as Saul realised he, alongside others who were without salvation, would be in danger of the judgement of God. Doubtless Saul in his ignorance believed he was doing the work of God but this was wrapped up in the falsehood of religion.

The example here is when a person is encountered by the power from on high you don't remain the same person, you become a new person in Christ. God saw in Saul a great potential to serve Him, one who would be given some hearing particularly as he was known to many for the past work he was engaged in as unsavoury as it was. The church of the day would find it very difficult to deny the change in the man now named Paul. A servant of the Most High God.

Saul needed the forgiveness of Christ to be fitted for the mission; he was now to become the preacher of the gospel to the Jews and gentiles alike. If this had not been the experience Saul had then he would never have found the truth about the cross and the resurrection of Jesus. God didn't see Saul as an obstacle but a potential for the kingdom. If you ever feel you are useless and have nothing to offer then STOP and ask God to forgive you for such blindness. If you believe this you are listening to a lie. Satan is the father of lies and wants you to think you are useless and have nothing to offer. Just like Saul, get up, dust yourself down and go forward in the name of Jesus seeking after His will for your life.

Obligation of the church today

How easy it is to get lost in a crowd, not to be seen or not to stand out. I remember as a young teenager that summed me up. I went to church to sit at the back to see my friends and plan the social activities for the week ahead. Little did I realise that on one Sunday God sent a messenger, it seemed, just to speak to me and my brother Dave who was by my side. He had pretty much the same agenda as me, thinking about the week ahead. The message that Sunday spoke about our obligation as Christians to serve the Lord. I remember the preacher pointing his finger right at us that seemed to pierce our hearts. The message was so strong: 'What will you do for Jesus who has done so much for you?' It was one of those spotlight moments when everything around you seemed dark but the space you occupied. I wanted the floor to open up and help me escape, but undeniably this was the moment God wanted to speak to me and my brother. The service came to an end and all I could do was to get outside of the church as quickly as possible; little did I realise my brother was right behind me. His first words to me were, 'Well, what are we going to do about it?'

My response was, 'I don't know, what can we do?'

A few days went by and we were still under the same conviction, what are we going to do about the preacher's message that had become all of a sudden so personal? Eventually we decided to talk about forming a gospel singing group, but there was a hitch: neither of us could play an instrument, neither of us could read music. We still couldn't escape the power of the preacher's message. What we realised is that the message was so personal – not only were we meant to be at that meeting but we were meant to hear the words of the preacher. God had made it clear; we had an obligation because of the cross of Jesus and the message of the gospel that bought both of us to the Lord.

We realised we were part of a bigger picture. The Bible says in Romans 12 that there are many members that make up the church and we all have different functions. I was so relieved to read that because I thought no matter what, we had a purpose to fulfil, even if it wasn't what was in our own minds. So many are just too comfortable to come to church and sit back and let others do all the work. I believe the obligation on all of us who call ourselves Christians is to serve the Lord.

The danger is church can become a club, a place just to socialise with no other demand on our lives. Romans 12:6 says, '*Having then gifts differing according to the grace that is given to us, let us use them*' (NKJV). You may never find out what your real gift or calling is until you find the giver. If everybody in all our churches operated the gifts that are available in Christ then the world would be a very different place. Six years later, God's touch on our lives showed us what God can do when we say 'yes Lord'. We bought guitars and amplifiers; we didn't know how to play them so we learnt a few chords and before we knew it, we were on the road going to other churches and singing, giving testimony and sharing the Word of God. Were we ready for this? In ourselves no, but in Christ all things are possible. It had to be for us 'all things although seemingly impossible are possible' (see Matthew 19:26). The real revelation was that we were not in our own strength anymore, something had taken over or someone had taken control. We had to learn it's not our strength but the work of the Holy Spirit in us that provides all we need to do the will of God here on earth.

This was just the beginning; there were mountain-top experiences, there were valley experiences, all of which were there to remind us that this was God's plan not our agenda we were working to. Over the period of six years we did things and went places that we never thought possible, but more importantly we were taken to locations to meet people that needed to hear about the love of Christ and how He would make a difference for them, forgiving sins and setting them free of the burden of sin. Later in this book I will share some of the stories of people whose lives were completely changed through the message of the gospel that we were privileged to share.

The main theme of this chapter is to remind us of our obligation in responding to the call of God. Don't assume because of your age or circumstances that you can't be useful to the Lord. But more importantly find out what you are meant to be doing at this juncture of your life whether young or old.

The apostle Paul reminds Timothy in scripture not to neglect the gift that was given to him when he became a Christian. God had equipped Timothy to accomplish the work he wanted him to do for the kingdom. There are times when we need to stir this gift up to make sure we are using it to its full potential.

What we seem to forget is it's not our strength that produces the fruit from our gifts but that of God through the Holy Spirit. I'm not just talking about the gifts of the Holy Spirit but the unique gift God gave you to minister for Him, which may be different to others, but will still glorify God. Remember, '"*Not by might nor by power, but by my Spirit*," *says the* Lord.' Besides the obligation on the individual in the church there is a collective responsibility we have to those around us and those who for the first time come into our churches. The place we call our spiritual home should be the most welcoming place for anybody to enter. A safe place, a place of warmth and love, a place of security and of hope.

When Jesus came into my life everything was going to change as long as I didn't try to take control back on my terms. If we really mean business with God don't just sing the words 'I surrender all'; make sure with the help of the Holy Spirit you apply these words each day of your life. Surrender doesn't mean you are giving up your whole identity; it means you are displaying your new identity in Jesus. Be the person He wants you to be, one of power, one who has a life full of the Holy Spirit to do the will of God in your neighbourhood and community. Our obligation is first to make sure we are available to hearing the Word of God and then responding to the Word so that as our lives change they will display the love of Jesus in a very needy world today. If God can do what He did through my brother and me, He can surely do the same and more through you. The time of listening to all the doubts and fears that have prevented you from going forward has to end. Now is your time to rise up and serve the Lord to do the impossible and release the gift of God's potential in you.

It all begins in each individual

When Jesus commissioned His disciples, He said, '*Therefore go and make disciples of all nations, baptising them in the name of the Father and of the Son and of the Holy Spirit, and teaching them to obey everything I have commanded you. And surely I am with you always, to the very end of the age*' (Matthew 28:19-20).

What an amazing promise, not just to the disciples but to you and me also. One of the reasons I love the Lord is that He doesn't deal with us on block; He sees us as unique individuals with all the potential in the world to serve Him.

You may not see this as an attraction, especially if it means being taken out of your comfort zone. But that's exactly what God wants to do to show you and help you understand how important you are to the plan of salvation. You may put up all the arguments you can think of why you shouldn't do what the Lord wants of you and why somebody else is better suited. Well, that may be because you have a low self-esteem, you may lack confidence, you may just be reserved and shy. Remember when Paul said to Timothy, 'Neglect not the gift within you' (1 Timothy 4:14), he was reminding Timothy that no longer did he have to see himself as he was but to see the new Timothy in Christ. Many of us are not naturally good at many things, but God sees the new abilities that come when the Holy Spirit takes over. Moses was a reluctant servant for God, Jonah was a reluctant servant for God, some of the prophets of old were reluctant servants of God; nevertheless God used them all to great effect.

Allow yourself the joy of meeting the Saviour Jesus on a one-to-one, in a quiet place, a private place and ask God to give your life a complete overhaul to the point of allowing Him to reshape what time you have left on this earth for Him. Don't put up the excuses or look for obstacles; place your life afresh in God's hands and let Him show you His plan for your life.

I promise you, God will not disappoint you. He will show you amazing things when you surrender to Him. So, stop looking in the mirror and seeing what you see but look upwards and see what God sees in you.

One of my Bibles sets out some practical advice on being a worker for God and I want to share some of these points with you. Remember Saul? A man who was bent on persecuting those who loved Christ and knew He was alive. Because Saul in his former state could not see this or believe it, all he wanted to do was to persecute those believers for their faith. What a change when Jesus came into his life. Here was possibly a hard man without too much time for his fellow man unless they conformed to his way of thinking, one you might say who had a heart of stone. But when Jesus came in . . .

If you are prepared to step out and serve God you will find your whole demeanour will change, you will have compassion like you never had before, you will have concern like you never had before, all of which makes contact with others far more reaching and easier to engage. You will find a natural desire to want to engage with others; you will all of a sudden be bold in your witnessing and you will have a freedom you never had before.

When God spoke to my brother and me many years ago it was through a preacher who maybe had to go through the early years of preparation before he was ready to preach. It was clear to us that his delivery of the message was not in his strength, but the power of God who spoke that evening. We certainly never expected the things in our lives to change like they did. God not only changed our way of thinking but changed our hearts. Instead of pleasing ourselves it was more about pleasing the Father in heaven.

Something else that changed was our perspective of other people. We found that we had a compassion for others that didn't exist before; we found we had concerns for others and wanted the best for them in Christ.

We came across such words as intercession and the importance of this being a part of our spiritual life, particularly our prayer life. Our whole perspective on life was changing with the sole purpose of seeing souls won for Christ. We wanted to sing for God, we needed to pray for souls to be saved all because of what had happened inside of us. It was not to be contained!

There is an amazing account of the power of prayer and praise together in Acts 16:25-34. I just love this account as it is such an inspiration. Here Paul is found in prison with Silas for preaching the gospel, so what do they do? They start praying and singing at midnight. Even in this situation they didn't let the bars of the prison stop them from sharing the love of Christ. When a Christian prays, he or she has heaven's attention, nothing will stop or prevent that which is directed to God getting through. They certainly had the prisoners' attention, for what was about to happen was going to shake the place apart. This was no freak accident but a powerful demonstration of God's response to a call from His servants. The Bible says that there was a great earthquake that tore the prison walls down, opened all the doors of the prison cells and even loosed the chains the prisoners were wearing. Imagine the chaos this would have caused in normal circumstances. No wonder the jailer wanted to commit suicide with all the prisoners escaping. But these were not normal circumstances; these were supernatural circumstances orchestrated from heaven. Paul calls out to the prison guard and tells him not to harm himself as all the prisoners were intact. Not only do Paul and Silas have the joy of leading this man to the Lord, but he then took Paul and Silas home to meet the family, have a meal and they all got saved. Who says God can't work through the individual? Paul and Silas didn't know what was going to happen that night but they believed in the One who makes it happen.

It's accounts like these that inspire and drive us on as Christians knowing that God is not only in control but is working His purposes out for all to come under the sound of the gospel message. Remember Christ died for all and it is not in His plan for any man to perish. I believe Paul and Silas were thanking God for the opportunities they had to share the love of Christ. It started in an individual and it still requires individuals to start responding to the call of God on their lives to be a people of compassion and concern for the souls of others.

Nothing comes without a cost

We all like a bargain, even better if it's free! But often something cheap or free can be something that doesn't last long. We are in a materialistic world where items that look like the real thing are in fact replicas and not the genuine thing. This is not the way heaven deals with us. As we have discovered, God's gifts to us are free, but they came with a cost to Jesus. Suffice to say, if there is also cost to us, it will mean sacrifice! Jesus paid for our redemption through the sacrifice upon the cross. If we are to take hold of the gifts that are available to us in the Holy Spirit then that may cost us. Just as some who you share the gospel with will not be able to surrender to the gift of eternal life simply because the cost to them is too great. It is not God's intention that one should be lost from eternity, yet those who feel they can't give up what they possess for the sake of salvation will not see heaven.

We live in a very materialistic world today where possessions are more important than anything else. There is an irony about this: we might have things today but we can't take them with us when we die. I referred to this earlier in the book. Rather than considering the call of the gospel, folk would rather put up reasons or excuses why they can't or don't want to give anything up. Many Christians today would rather keep one foot in the world and the other in church just in case. There are no half-way measures. Jesus says in Matthew 12:30 'Whoever is not with me is against me.' Christ gave His all. Surely that's the least we should give back to Him for our salvation through the cross. I remember as a small boy the road to school seemed so long. Each morning we would go the same route yet on rainy days it seemed even longer. It was only when I grew up and walked the same route that it became clear that the journey was in fact only a few hundred metres. In other words, my perspective changed as I grew older. It's a little like this when we get to know the Lord; given time to grow in the knowledge of His Word and learning to commune with our heavenly Father put's a whole new perspective on why God loved me so much and why He didn't want me to miss out on the blessings He had already prepared for me.

So, you may ask what is the cost to me?

To begin with you must look at your lifestyle and ask yourself, does it reflect Jesus in me? Am I an example to bring glory to God through the way I live? Is my personality and character one that stands out among the crowd? Remember we are not called to be all things to all men, but what we are called to be is available to share the love of God with all the world. One of the things that struck me when Billy Graham came to my home city of Bristol was his whole team seemed fully committed to their mission. They had a real compassion for the lost and a real desire to serve the Lord however they could. It was clear to me that they lived the life that was changed by the Spirit of God;

they wanted people to be introduced to Jesus by their example. Furthermore, they demonstrated a love for the people they had come to reach. Billy Graham was fully committed to his calling that became apparent in the uncompromising gospel of Jesus and the cross that he preached night after night. I believe the response to the gospel was not because of Billy Graham as an individual, but the work of the Holy Spirit using a servant of God to proclaim the good news of the gospel. In the human sense the cost to all ministers and evangelists is often far greater than most will ever know, not just the physical and mental cost but the human sacrifice as well. For many of the team it would mean a lengthy time away from loved ones and family, it may mean personal hidden costs that only the Lord knows about. But clearly it was their calling that drove them forward and the joy of leading folk to Christ. You may wonder sometimes why God leads us a particular way in life. It may be through our career or work circumstances that lead to much greater things totally unrelated to the original journey we set out on, but, nonetheless, God is still there leading and guiding us through to the destination He has set out for us. When we say 'yes' to God regardless of the unknown, we can be sure our lives will have a whole new meaning, but be sure it will come with a cost. One that has a reward that will be everlasting.

Not my will but Thy will be done

When Jesus walked this earth He made it very clear that He was about His Father's will. He was not on some egotistical journey to impress men but He clearly came into the world to glorify the Father in obedience to His calling. Because Jesus was God in the flesh He could have just carried on as though it was all about Him. But this was not at all the point of His coming. He came with a specific purpose, mission and ministry. Up to this point the people lived under an imperfect Law, and now was the time for grace and mercy to abound in Christ. There is a much wider and deeper expounding of this area of scripture which demands further and greater explanation than is the purpose of this book.

The principle is to acknowledge that when we are called to do the work of God, it is not about what we have to offer but about what Christ has to offer those who are seeking Him. We are the instrument in God's hands operating under the guidance of the Holy Spirit to accomplish the will of the Father; we are the channel that God uses to bring men and women under the sound of the gospel of redemption, love and forgiveness. When we operate under the supernatural power of the Holy Spirit then we will see the fruit of our ministry and calling.

Many people go to church but are totally blind to the truth of the Word; they have worked it all out by themselves. Their future is based on being seen to be respectable in the eyes of man, thinking, 'I am good enough as I am' or 'I'm as good as any other'. Jesus didn't come to earth to live by comparisons, He came to live by the standards God had already set. Man by his own standards is sinful, it's in his nature. God sent Jesus to show there is a better way. Why not meet the one who personified the heart of God, who showed the very nature of a loving God not wanting anybody to perish or die without hope? How many of us take note of what we say when we say the Lord's prayer? 'Thy will be done as it is in heaven.' God's will is for eternal benefit not for gaining respectability from man.

CHAPTER FIVE

WHY IS IT SO DIFFICULT?

I'm the one who's been wronged

I'm sure we have all heard the phrase 'I will never forgive you for what you have done'. If ever there was a statement that causes so much trouble in life whether as a Christian or not, then this one ranks high up the list. What happens here is that statements like these, whether meant or not, can be the cause of the biggest breakdown of relationships in our communities. Often those who speak out these words have no idea what they are saying, particularly when it comes to the consequential effects that could scar a person for life, besides putting a huge burden on the person who made the statement. Without going into a psychological explanation of what unforgiveness is as seen by the scientific and medical world, I want to concentrate what the Bible has to say. However, one thing we can agree on is the fact that unforgiveness will manifest itself in the imbalance it causes to our physical bodies.

Anger, frustration, hatred that can often lead to violence are just some of the responses that are associated with unforgiveness. It is said that unforgiveness has a direct impact on the mental health and psychology of a person.

In short, we allow the normal balance of the mind to be interrupted by this added stress response that interferes with our personality. Right at the beginning of the book of Romans there is a very sad but real situation that still exists today: men will not give up ungodly and unrighteous things. *'For the wrath of God is revealed from heaven against all ungodliness and unrighteousness of men, who hold the truth in unrighteousness'* (Romans 1:18 KJV). Man decided that they had a better way than God's way. Sin is very real and has a corrupting and debilitating effect on mankind. One word that stands out in the sad list of unrighteous acts of men in verse 31 is 'unforgiveness'. For so many Christians today unforgiveness is the biggest hindrance to them growing in Christ and realising their full potential in God.

There are of course different paths one can take when it comes to unforgiveness. You can either believe that you have been so wronged that your unforgiveness is justified or you can adopt this stance simply because you don't know another way. Either way you may not escape the burden it puts on you even subconsciously. The problem is that until you want it to change or go away it won't; it will always be there festering away and causing amongst other things hardness of heart. Unforgiveness is like passing judgement on a person. What happens is that the load of guilt is laid on the other person and condemns them to carry that load for the rest of their lives. You may feel justified in doing this especially if the act caused you so much pain and maybe even loss. Yet we cannot escape the fact that unforgiveness is a sin and needs to be addressed not only for ourselves but also for the other party. For many, to forgive another who has caused much pain and hurt is possibly the most difficult thing they will have to deal with in their Christian experience, but the one thing we cannot escape is the fact that the Bible says, '*If you do not forgive others their sins, your Father will not forgive your sins*' (Matthew 6:15).

There have been many accounts where some Christians have found it in their hearts to forgive some of the most heinous crimes committed by man. For such a response something has to happen deep within the heart of the victim. Remember we said earlier in these pages that Jesus came to set the captive free. The captive can be the victim as well as the guilty party. God is wanting to show us a way to complete freedom in such circumstances. Where you feel you are the one who's been wronged, may I suggest you take a step back for a moment and think about the positives that could come out of you taking an action that would to the world seem unimaginable? Our first instinct is to want revenge or some sort of compensation but what does that produce in the long term? Does it mean the hurt and pain will go away? Doubtful, there is a real need for healing of the situation to take place and if you are the one who is not forgiving then it has to start in you.

Say sorry – why?

Even if you are not the injured party who is finding it difficult to forgive, saying sorry can have such a healing effect on the part of the other person. So often we have no idea what the injured party has been through although they are the one holding on to unforgiveness. Rest assured, if we are talking about a Christian who is trying to go on with the Lord, holding on to unforgiveness is going to affect their whole being not just physically but mentally and spiritually as well.

Warren Wiersbe says that there is a big difference between hurting somebody and harming somebody. He was referring to the situation in the church at Corinth (2 Corinthians 2:5-11) where an issue amongst the believers had not been dealt with but had divided the church. Paul in this case was the injured party.

Because of the seriousness of the sin and accusation against Paul's authority, Paul wrote to the church and said the issue must be dealt with. The major point here is that Paul's letter was written with compassion and love that displayed the nature of Christ, encouraging the church to restore the man in question. The reason we should be prepared to say sorry is to see the bigger picture. If we obey the Word not only will we be able to act accordingly as prompted by the Holy Spirit, but we will see the fruit of our actions in the restoration of what otherwise is a broken friendship or harmed fellowship. Saying sorry can be a powerful testimony especially as it will help others grow in their relationship with God and ultimately with others. Paul goes on to say, '*You ought rather to forgive and comfort him, lest perhaps such a one be swallowed up with too much sorrow. Therefore I urge you to reaffirm your love to him*' (v. 7-8 NKJV). Forgiveness helps to heal a hurt and broken heart. I have personally known experiences like this in my own life where a person had been hurt by me but I was completely unaware of it for years! They were carrying this hurt for such a long time and it was only when they made it known that I was able to say sorry for something that I had not consciously done. I realised that saying sorry healed and restored the situation. The hurt was no longer a hurt; saying sorry avoided any lasting harm.

There may be occasions when you are called on more than once to deal with similar situations. Remember love forgives and forgets. Don't let saying sorry be the cause of ongoing broken relationships or fellowship even if you are not the injured party.

I feel too hurt to let go

If on the other hand you are the injured party, does that give you the right to hold on to hurt and unforgiveness? Too many people today are spiritually handicapped by unforgiveness, they either won't or can't forgive the perpetrator of the problem. Often the immediate effect of any cause of hurt or harm can express itself in anger, revenge or even violence, none of which is synonymous with the Christian character-building that should be seen as we grow in the Lord.

Hebrews chapter 3 speaks about the condition of the heart. There is a popular saying, 'The heart of every problem is the problem of the heart.' The danger of being hurt is to allow your heart to harden towards the other person or party. Hebrews 3:12 says, '*Beware, brethren, lest there be in any of you an evil heart of unbelief in departing from the living God*' (NKJV). Just as the children of Israel had hardened their hearts against God, He didn't fail them but they certainly failed God. Is the hurt we feel when we have been badly wronged so overwhelming that our initial feelings won't go away and we can't move forward? Shall we just accept the burden and carry on as it's not our fault but that of another? Letting go of anything is not always easy and often takes time, but unless we do, we will find ourselves in a self imposed prison of misery and loss of joy.

What we are being asked to do through the Word of God is not easy because it's contrary to our fleshy nature; our first reaction for any hurt is to want revenge. But this is not the way God wants us to go; He wants to do something in us that will make a lasting change and have a better outcome.

Remember the scripture, '*Come to me, all you who are weary and burdened, and I will give you rest*' (Matthew 11:28).

During the days of our ministry as a gospel group we were invited to a number of prisons to sing and testify of the goodness of God. On one occasion we had just finished the concert at a high-security prison not far from our homes when a prison officer came up to us and asked if we would go and meet a prisoner in his cell who wanted to come to the concert but had a panic attack that prevented him attending. We agreed to this request and a couple of us went to meet this man. I will never forget this meeting; as we entered the cell under the watchful eye of the prison officer the man who was in prison for a very serious crime cowered in the corner of his cell. The officer stepped forward to suggest we leave but the man asked us to stay. I very slowly approached the man with my hand out in a gesture of friendship to show him we were no threat to him.

After a short while of silence, we managed to learn from the prisoner what he had done to reduce him to this weak and frail person after being in prison for some time with a stretch still to come.

When speaking to him he said something to me that saddened my heart. He said, 'Once a con always a con.' This man knew no other way than committing crime! In other words, he didn't know how to let go. He blamed society for not helping him to mend his ways after a number of previous convictions and spells in prison.

We shared the love of Jesus with this man in the hope that one day he would see that there is another way to deal with hurt even if you are the one who is guilty. We came across many other situations where the hopelessness of any future for these men seemed so bleak. On some occasions we did see some respond to the gospel and thankfully, due to other Christians regularly attending prison services, were glad to know they were going on with the Lord.

Even perpetrators who are the cause of hurt and pain can also suffer the consequences of unforgiveness. Sometimes their guilt will not let them go and they are trapped in their own wrongdoing.

The scar won't go away

I often think of when Jesus spoke to Thomas and invited him to see His body, to examine the nail prints in His hands and the spear wound in His side to put to rest Thomas' doubting that He was the Christ.

I like to think that a scar is not a reminder of the pain but the mark of healing that has taken place. So many folks are trapped by the former thought relating to pain rather than seeing the body healed. This is also a problem with the mind when we only allow our thinking to concentrate on the negative aspect of a past problem. Sometimes we don't realise we are the problem that prevents healing taking place. We say 'I can forgive, but I can't forget'. Imagine if that was the position Christ took with us concerning our sin; it would completely nullify the work of Calvary if this were the case.

Don't let the scar of the past hurts and pain prevent you from receiving the release that comes through healing.

Scarring is the natural process towards healing and in some cases it can be eradicated over time. This is often true of how things happen in our spiritual lives; not everything will necessarily go away instantly – depending on how deep the wound, the length of time for healing to take place can be drawn out particularly in the physical sense – but this does not prevent us from moving forward and realising the power in forgiveness that will bring healing at a different pace, allowing the Spirit of God to work in us.

When you next look at the scar or the problem that has caused the hurt in you, remember Christ is able to deal with every situation, there is nothing too hard for Him. As long as the scar exists it can either be a blessing when you have given it back to the Lord to deal with or it can be the biggest stumbling block in your spiritual growth. Don't allow the expression of our minds to be manifest in the misuse of our tongues. Think on before you allow your mind to control your tongue.

Proverbs 15:33 says, '*The fear of the Lord is the instruction of wisdom*; *and before honour is humility*' (KJV). What am I saying here? We can often convince ourselves that we are so right and that justifies our excuse for not allowing the scar to heal. This last verse in Proverbs 15 talks about the fear of the Lord, the blessings that come from the fear of the Lord encourage us to recognise evil when it comes; it also reminds us that we should depart from evil. You may not think your position of harbouring a hurt or pain caused by another is justified, but the Word of God reminds us that there is no profit in such a stance. In Proverbs 16:2 we read, '*All a person's ways seem pure to them, but motives are weighed by the Lord.*' It's easy to think that our own self-righteousness is clean simply because we have convinced ourselves. The Bible says the Lord looks on the heart and judges our motives from there! When the Lord takes control, not only will the scar heal but it will disappear and not condition our mind to the past allowing the trap of pain to continue. Turning anger to love is not part of human nature, but it is part of the supernatural power of God to work in us. Over the years there have been a large number of times when there have been stories on the national news of people being harmed, hurt or murdered and family members have stepped forward to forgive the guilty party. This isn't the normal nature of man, but it is the normal nature of God in man. The scar will remain as long as you want it to; you are able to deal with this when you give it over to the Lord with a heart of forgiveness.

I believe I'm in the right

As long as you feel you are right and everybody else is wrong then there is a problem that may never go away! Often stubbornness or pride are very dangerous attitudes to allow a foothold in anyone. Particularly pride. The Bible says, *'Pride goes before destruction'* (Proverbs 16:18). No good comes from pride in Proverbs 11:2: *'Pride comes, then comes shame.'* No matter what the situation you must consider what's behind your motive. If your pride is controlling you then it will be all the more difficult to deal with any issue that is holding you back from the blessings the Lord has in store.

In the Old Testament the people of Israel missed out so much on the blessings of God due to stubbornness and pride; they thought they knew best. The Lord appeared to

Solomon one night and said to him, '*If my people who are called by my name, will humble themselves and pray and seek my face and turn from their wicked ways, then I will hear from heaven, and will forgive their sin, and will heal their land*' (2 Chronicles 7:14). Is it just possible that in our own experiences we are also missing out on the blessings of God due to pride preventing the release of God's power in our lives to overcome the enemy?

Who is telling you that you are in the right when actions that reflect the Lord in your life and who should be guiding you by His Holy Spirit, is being pushed to the back? Pride builds walls that sometimes seem impregnable; it makes us feel untouchable because we don't want anybody to tell us we are wrong or there is another way.

James 4:6-7 says, '*God opposes the proud, but shows favour to the humble. Submit yourselves, then, to God. Resist the devil, and he will flee from you.*' Scripture reminds us that pride is part of our sinful nature and has no place in the renewed character of the Christian. Notice that in every situation we are encouraged to take the action which in turn makes a loud statement to the devil who is trying to rob us of all identity in Christ. Whether you believe you are right or not, holding on to a grudge especially between Christians who should take every opportunity to fellowship, then we are on our own. Why do we carry the burden of hurt and allow pride to dictate the outcome?

Years ago, we used to sing a song that says:

Christ is the answer to my every need;
Christ is the answer, He is my friend indeed.
Problems of life my spirit may assail, with Christ my
Saviour
I need never fail, for Christ is the answer to my need.

The consequence of stubbornness or pride can be spiritual blindness. In this instance it means we cannot see where we are wrong in our thinking and actions, even when they dishonour God. It can also mean we are not allowing our spiritual understanding of the truth to take precedence in such cases. When somebody who you might trust comes alongside you to say you might be wrong, this blindness can also be the cause of a breakdown in fellowship and friendship, especially if you don't accept their friendship and council. It should become apparent that no matter what we feel it will come down to surrender to Christ if we believe the words of the song we've just read. Who else could we call on to get us out of this mess of emotion that has a grounding but need not have a firm foundation?

I can't see an impasse

Because we can't see a problem doesn't mean the problem has gone away. You may have been able to put it to the back of your mind for the time being but rest assured it is still there until it is dealt with. We read in God's Word to not let the sun go down on our wrath (Ephesians 4:26). If there's something to be dealt with today, do it. Don't leave it to fester a night or a day longer. Blindness of spirit can also cause a hardening of the heart. Paul, writing to the church in Rome, tells the Christians not to be ignorant of God's plan for His people, *'lest you should be wise in your own opinion, that blindness in part has happened to Israel'* (Romans 11:25 NKJV).

The people of Israel were stuck in their old ways; they hadn't come into the full understanding that the old Laws were abolished by the cross of Calvary and all that was accomplished there. To some degree they were trapped in their own understanding and not yet freed by the grace of God. Some Jews today still can't see beyond their traditions. In 2 Corinthians 3:13-17 the Bible speaks of a spiritual veil that has covered the sight of the Jews, not just over their eyes but their hearts as well. Religion had become a distraction and a diversion from the truth.

Just as God promised never to desert His people Israel, neither will He let you go because of your situation or condition of your heart; this won't stop Him from loving you or seeking after you to show you a better way. God says when the heart is turned towards Him the blindness and hardening of the heart will be dealt with once and for all if we stay close to Him. When we are trying to work out our own salvation, let alone the problems of life, the Bible speaks of us as in darkness. Well, this couldn't be truer. How many of us grope around not knowing which way to turn, especially when we find ourselves in trouble of one kind or another?

We are reminded in Ephesians 5:8, *'For you were once darkness, but now you are light in the Lord. Walk as children of light'* (NKJV).

I remember when I was in Israel on a visit with some German friends, we were invited to a Bible school just outside of Jerusalem. We were greeted with such warmth by the man in charge of the school. When I had the opportunity to talk to this man alone, who I had already assumed was a Christian Jew, he surprised me and told me he was a born-again Spirit-filled Christian Arab. He was called to work in this place to share the truth of the scripture with Jews – how about that? When God steps in and we are willing to let go and give God control then all things are possible.

I shall never forget the humility of this man and the love of Jesus that shone through his personality.

If we are content to stay in our blindness (darkness) then we may never reach the level of fulfilment and joy God has in store for us. Ask God to open your eyes to see the impasse and then pray that this obstacle be removed. Being stuck in blindness is being in bondage. Christ has come to set us free from such debilitating conditions; Jesus came to set the captive free.

If you can't see an impasse ask God to set you free to see the light of the truth of situations that need to be dealt with for Jesus' sake and His glory.

CHAPTER SIX

DO I GO FIRST?

For many people the thought of being the first to step up to any challenge is a daunting thing, and in this case maybe even more challenging if we have to do something that is completely out of character. Going back to my gospel group days, if my brother and I together with one other friend had said 'no' to the call of God then we would never have experienced the blessings along the way. It was certainly out of character for me to want to be at the front of a stage or platform singing and sharing my faith. I was a young Christian, very inexperienced and needing to learn a lot! I felt untrained, inadequate and not particularly eloquent, so how on earth did God see in any of us the ability to do what we knew He had called us to? What soon became apparent was that whatever we did was not in our strength. After many of the services and events we attended we used to sit back and wonder what happened, especially when we had the joy of seeing people come to Christ as a result of our ministry. We soon realised it was not our strength that carried us through but the power of the Holy Spirit working in us.

Many years ago we were asked to go to play at a gospel concert in a small village on Salisbury Plain in Wiltshire. This was after a day's work for all of us and it was in the

Autumn, the night was dark and wet, we didn't have satnavs to help us find the way, still we carried on through the dark and the rain towards our destination. I remember whilst on the road the rain was lashing down and visibility was very poor. The journey seemed to take an age. As we were nearing our destination I hit a flooded section of the road that transported my car across to the oncoming lane. Frantically I managed to steer back to the right side of the road to continue our journey. Needless to say, we arrived a little late at the village hall. It was packed out and yet there seemed to be a really strange air in the place. We hurriedly set up our equipment ready to play but not before the speaker for the evening asked us to go and pray in the side room before we commenced our set.

The speaker that night was a man named Doug Barnett. He told us that we had come to this place to share the gospel but on this night there would be real opposition to what we were about to present in song and word. He informed us that there were practising witches present who were against the gospel being preached.

This was a first for us, yet we knew we were there for a purpose much higher and greater than the powers of darkness that had already tried to prevent us from attending this meeting.

We prayed that God would not only have the victory that night but we would stand against the powers of darkness in Jesus' name. As we commenced our singing and testifying there were moments of stony silence. We realised we had a choice: either to stand down or go on with what we were called to do. After about thirty-five minutes we took a break at which time the three witches at the rear of the room were making as much noise and fuss as possible, trying to stir up some kind of trouble. We took our break again in the little side room and spent the time praying before we were back on.

Stepping back on the platform it seemed even colder in the room and I remember that the Word of God said we had nothing to fear. Jesus said, '*I am with you always*' – that was good enough for us. We then did something that in our own strength we could not have otherwise done; we confronted the witches directly at the back and told them that we were there to bring hope and light to those who were seeking the love of Christ. We bound the activities of the power of darkness and proclaimed Jesus as Lord. Very soon after the three witches left the hall rather quickly! That night we saw as a result of the work of the Holy Spirit, people come to Christ, some of whom said they were being encouraged to join in with the practices of the local coven and other deeds of darkness. The reason for sharing this occasion is to encourage you to step up to being first, not in your strength but in the strength of the Lord. What started out to be a night for spreading the gospel turned out to be a night to instruct us and help us grow in Jesus because we were prepared to go first!

Sacrifice is costly

An example of sacrifice is when something precious is wilfully given up. We know from scripture that under the old system people would bring offerings to the priest to sacrifice on their behalf for the atonement of sin; whatever the offering, whether a small or large animal, it was a cost to the giver. Today, sacrifice is giving up something that will have a cost to you – it may be time or money, even possessions –

whatever it is it will be at a cost to the giver. Sacrifice is also about letting go, letting go of the things that we hold dear or regard as something of value to us whether good or bad!

When I look back in scripture and think of when Jesus asked the disciples to follow Him, there was sacrifice on behalf of what they were leaving behind to do such a thing. What they didn't know at the time was the real cost of that sacrifice.

In a similar way, when we are called to do something that is difficult for us to do but we know at the same time is the right thing to do, then this too can be done sacrificially. Going back to Hebrews 10 we read about the supreme sacrifice that Jesus made for us. Remember the tokens of sacrifice under the old Law could not take away sin. Only the blood of God's own Son could do this, the spotless Lamb of God – Jesus.

We may not be asked to lay down our life as many have in the past either for the sovereign of their country or for other convicting beliefs. At the time of writing this book we are experiencing a worldwide pandemic, a virus that has claimed tens of thousands of lives in the UK alone. A cost that none of us would willingly want to make. Yet there are times in our lives when we will be challenged about making some sort of sacrifice. In the context of this book it will most likely be to deal with issues that benefit another. If you are willing to let God take control of all situations then as part of our spiritual growth you will eventually see the purpose in this whole business of forgiveness. I think we have established the fundamental aspect of the need to forgive but to carry it out is another cost altogether.

Such was the revival recorded in Acts 2:45 that the Christians sold all their possessions. There were about

3,000 people added to the church through the preaching of the gospel by Peter. As you can imagine, having guests of about 3000 turn up at your church would put some into total turmoil, but here the church knew what to do. Because they had been taught that there were far more important things in life than possessions they gladly sold what possessions they had; this in itself was a sacrifice of love.

In ordinary circumstances it is unlikely that this would have happened, but a need was revealed and the call was answered. Sometimes what we are asked to do in the name of the Lord calls for extraordinary responses to extraordinary circumstances. The example in Acts also shows that situations like this can have a profound effect on those involved i.e. Acts 2:44-46 they *'had all things in common'* (KJV). What was going on here was the power of the Holy Spirit working in those believers who wanted to glorify God in their witness to others. When it comes to forgiveness, sure there will be a cost, but looking to the bigger picture the work that you could be part of will bring healing and glory to God in the process. Often before people can let go of anything there has to be a bit of soul searching to put things into perspective.

Looking inward

This is an area we all need to consider. In the first instance, how easy it is for us to be inward looking purely to convince us of our own justification for not doing anything. I remember as a young Christian somebody saying to me that I couldn't become a Christian because the Bible is full of what you can't do. Puzzled, I looked at this person and said, 'My understanding is that there are more "do's" in the Bible than "don'ts" so I'm not sure where you are coming from.' How Satan loves to confuse us by telling lies, particularly if it leads to the truth – because we know that the truth sets us free. Looking inward can be very revealing if you are open to being honest about yourself. There are only two that know the real you, that is the Lord and you. So when you take an honest look at yourself, remember there is one who knows you better than you know yourself.

Looking inward should reveal the real you, it should show you the condition of your heart – not your pumping heart but the heart that was changed when you surrendered to Christ as Lord and Saviour. If you are struggling to forgive someone then examine the heart that can reveal the love of Jesus and all that it means to bring healing and health into a situation.

Too many want to give an impression that will make them look good. Jesus said in Matthew 7:15, '*Beware of false prophets, who come to you in sheep's clothing, but inwardly they are ravenous wolves*' (NKJV). Don't do anything in the name of the Lord that puts on a false face; even if those around you can't see the real you, God can. I recall a time when my brother and I, who because of closeness in years looked alike, were both sat at the front of a service one day when the speaker who knew us both said in his message, 'I know the two boys sat in the front row, or do I? They could be wearing masks.' The message struck me as it made me think of what impression I was giving to others concerning my life now given over to Jesus. It concerned me that I didn't want to be like the 'false prophets' because that would not honour God and show others the love of Jesus. Looking inward can be costly, it may even surprise you to the point of realisation that something is lacking. If forgiveness is to come, I believe the heart must be right before God; if we choose to go it alone then we are wide open to failure: not only will the person that you want to forgive see through you, but God will also see through you.

There is an old hymn we used to sing with words that are timeless;

> Search me, O God, and know my heart today,
> Try me, O Saviour, know my thoughts, I pray;
> See if there be some wicked way in me;
> Cleanse me from every sin, and set me free.

Maybe looking inward is too important not to miss before we put forgiveness into action!

Why is it so important to look inward? What you are doing is looking at your heart, it is here the Bible says that pride is conceived (Deuteronomy 8:14) – we have already alluded to this earlier in the book. Another reason is to test your motives. If your heart is not right how can you ever deal with the heart of the problem? We should understand that God looks on the heart of man to see where he stands. Is your heart tempered by the Holy Spirit or is it still under your own control? It's easy to think that by keeping part of yourself you can opt in and out of the grace of God. The cross was not optional, your salvation is not optional; it's only you that makes it so. Proverbs 23:12 says, 'Apply your heart to instruction and your ears to the words of knowledge.' If our lives are to reflect the Lord then our hearts should obey the Word of God in the way we live and conduct ourselves. When you stop to think what is being asked of you to demonstrate the love of God, especially when you have to forgive, you come to the realisation that only you can do this, and yet you are not entirely alone!

I can't do this on my own

There is no situation God will ask you to conduct completely on your own; if you know in your heart you have to do something even though it may be very difficult for you, if it is something that will bring fruit and glorify God then rest assured you are certainly not on your own. The fact that you are challenged to sort out a situation that you know isn't right, and you have the key to putting it right, the way is set out by the Holy Spirit to bring healing, restoration and blessing. Jesus says to His disciples, '*I am with you always, to the very end of the age.*' We have the same promise the Holy Spirit is here to guide us and instruct us in the ways of God until Christ comes again. There are many times I think I can do things better than to ask anybody else to do them for me. I have had to learn over time that doesn't have to be the case. But in matters of life and certainly of the heart (spiritual) then I need all the help I can get! I am so thankful the Holy Spirit came to give me all the help I need.

Learning to hear the voice of the Holy Spirit is something that comes as we grow in Christ, just as a shepherd knows his sheep so the Lord knows us. It's only when we can say we know the Lord, that we can do all things in Him. Jesus is described in John 10 as the 'Good Shepherd'. It speaks of the relationship between the shepherd and the sheep (God and His people) clearly to express a unique relationship, one of love and compassion. We are known by God in every possible detail; no matter if we look alike, we are unique to Him. He understands us, He knows our weaknesses, our strengths, He knows our deep longings and desires but perhaps most important of all He knows our needs. There are no situations we are likely to face that God can't deal with. The longer we stay close to the Shepherd the safer we will be, we will also get to know Him and trust Him where ever He leads us.

When I think back over my 70 years of life, I can testify to the amazing love and compassion of Jesus my Lord. There have been many times when I thought I could go it alone only to find that I have fallen, let the Lord down and not lived the life that I could have, close to the Shepherd. The amazing thing is that just as the prodigal son realised he needed to return to his father, so did I. I love that part of the account where it says, *'While he was still a long way off, his father saw him and was filled with compassion for him; he ran to his son, threw his arms round him and kissed him'* (Luke 15:20). Did the son deserve this treatment? NO! Did I deserve the mercy and grace of God? NO! It says the Father saw me a long way off. Whatever the distance we put between us and the Lord it is never going to be too much for Him to see us and want us to return to Him. It's in this sense we are constantly on the mind of the Shepherd as He longs for us to trust Him no matter what the circumstances.

If you think you can't do something because you feel alone, then let me tell you, as far as God is concerned you are never alone when you put your trust in Him and call on His name to help you. His love for you far outweighs even the biggest obstacle you may face in your lifetime and He is there to help and guide you each step of the way.

How will I know what to say?

Whether we are approaching someone to seek forgiveness or whether we are to stand up and testify for the first time, we often see a blank sheet of paper before us because we don't know what to say or how to put the words together that will have meaning. To be sincere in your actions is one thing, but unless you are prepared for the actions you take, you can be sincerely wrong in your approach.

As a young Christian I was advised to be careful and prayerful about anything I did for the Lord, knowing that as I surrendered the problem to Him, He would guide and instruct me in His ways. There's a great chorus we sometimes sing;

Spirit of the living God, fall afresh on me.
Spirit of the living God, fall afresh on me.
Melt me, mould me, fill me, use me,
Spirit of the living God, fall afresh on me.

Here we find the amazing work of the Holy Spirit in our lives when we surrender to line three of this chorus. It's basically saying, take me out of myself and make me the person You see in me so that whatever I do is the reborn person in Jesus producing the fruit of Your Word in my life.

The Bible says, '*You shall receive power when the Holy Spirit has come upon you*' (Acts 1:8 NKJV). Don't let the fear of not being able to say the right words at the right time be your excuse for not fulfilling the action. The same power that helped, instructed and guided the early apostles is the same Holy Spirit today, it's His power that is available to you and me. God's precious Holy Spirit is there to empower us in so many ways and especially in specific instances.

Put your faith in action and allow the Holy Spirit to show you how to respond in situations that you would normally run away from. Remember, faith is a journey and we are not alone on this journey. God is there right by your side.

Does it mean digging up the past?

Many times in the past I have been asked to sit alongside others or share with others concerning a dispute or difference that has caused a breakdown in fellowship between the two parties. Ordinarily I would encourage them to try and deal with the situation themselves, but there are occasions when this just doesn't work. Matthew 5:23 tells us to deal with any difference against a brother or sister and not to let it fester. Sometimes it's difficult to do this on your own, but to trust and rely on the Holy Spirit is the way forward. Approaching the person that has caused you so much pain is not an easy thing to do but if we are to obey the Word of God and avoid this breakdown of friendship and fellowship, we must trust God in the situation. Unforgiveness is so debilitating and can rob us of joy and peace in our hearts and minds.

Another aspect of taking such an action is the fear of what may come out in conversation; this could cause a further reminder and stirring-up of the past. If your heart is right it's not about concentrating on the past but looking to the future mending and restoring rather than relieving yourself of further anger. In Matthew 18:20 Jesus reminds us that '*where two or three are gathered together . . . [He is] there in the midst of them*' (NKJV). It's worth remembering that in matters of the kingdom we are never alone, we don't have to feel there is any obligation to adopt a more righteous stance than anybody else. What purpose or profit is there in rehearsing the past when what you are trying to do is to forgive and forget the past and mend for the future. On one occasion, I remember a lady saying that to forgive someone who had caused her so much pain was like a huge weight being lifted from her; she had no more reason to carry this unwanted burden any longer, even though she was the injured party. She wanted to be free of the weight of unforgiveness in her heart and able to move forward and enjoy the fullness of what God had in store for her. Maybe if this book is speaking to you, NOW is the time to let go of the burden of unforgiveness that you may have been carrying for far too long.

I don't say lightly forget the past, because in our humanity that's not always so easy. But remember you don't have to keep digging it up to remind yourself or keep the weight of this hurt preventing you from doing the right thing in the eyes of the Lord.

When my children were very young and if on occasion they had hurt themselves, they would come in crying that they had fallen down and cut their leg or their arm. After cleaning them up we would say to them, 'Now don't touch – that needs time to heal.' Invariably they would come back a few days later and say, 'Daddy, my leg is not getting better. I picked the scab off and it's bleeding again.' Isn't this just like us sometimes? We keep picking at the scab – the place of the source of pain and hurt – to see if it's ever going to go away. I am so glad that when God says He will forgive us He also says, 'I will remember your sins no more.' He doesn't want us to be guilty of carrying the very thing that once separated us from Him. Now, when we have to forgive somebody, we have to do the same, let it go as though it never happened and don't hold it against that person any longer. You might say in the human sense that's not possible, but remember you are not acting alone. So don't do it, let the past and all the ugly detail go once and for all.

CHAPTER SEVEN

WHAT'S IN IT FOR ME?

When it comes to having to forgive someone, the real obstacle is often the introspective view we have of ourselves because we feel the hurt party, we want to think the outcome will still weigh things on our side to justify the way we feel and have felt. Some sort of 'I was in the right all along' feeling. As we have already discussed it can often be the situation that you are carrying more pain over the issue than is intended because you feel so hurt and you have allowed this hurt to grow and become more than it really is! Keeping things in perspective is vital to ensuring you are not allowing the influence of the adversary to keep you from the liberty of forgiveness.

For a moment let's suggest it's not only about you, but it involves two others that should matter in your life; on one account it involves the other person with which you have the problem and on the other it very much involves the Lord, if you have submitted your life to Him. The other person may be unaware of the problem unless you communicate this to them. But one thing is for sure, you will not be able to hide this from the Lord who knows you better than you know yourself.

Maybe, rather than ask the question, 'What's in it for me?' ask yourself, 'Is it all about me?' If we want the peace of God in this matter then we need to remind ourselves that it's not so much about me but how I can honour God and respond to the Holy Spirit's leading. The biggest block to any blessing from the Lord is us, usually because we try to do things in our own way and not God's. Constantly I am drawn back to the cross of Christ for the supreme example of sacrifice and love. Jesus loved us all even though we were far away from Him, the pain He bore to show us how much He loved us is beyond our understanding. You may have heard the phrase 'It was love that nailed Him to the cross, to suffer pain even when He was faultless'. Jesus would say to you, 'It wasn't about Me – it is all about you.' What a wonderful perspective to have.

The apostle Paul said in Philippians 2:3-4, '*Let nothing be done through selfish ambition or conceit, but in lowliness of mind let each esteem others better than himself. Let each of you look out not only for his own interests, but also for the interests of others*' (NKJV). Paul's encouragement here was to remind the church about the obligation to each other. Read this chapter to verse 16 and then consider how your life might reflect this. Right at the beginning of Philippians 2 Paul says, '*If there is any encouragement in Christ*' (ESV), reminding us why and who we are to represent in our conduct and witness day by day.

So, you ask, 'What's in it for me?' The reward for obedience is a treasure laid up in heaven; one day when we stand before the throne of grace we will have the joy of the fulfilment of the promises of God right there before us. I don't know what our crown of glory will look like, but I'm sure it will reflect the joy of the Father who sees the child who persevered.

It's all about me!

Clearly it's not all about you or me, it's about a much bigger plan than a self-centred view that is restricted to looking inward. Jesus died for all – the lovely, the unlovely, the good and the bad, old and young – no matter what your condition, no matter whether you are society's biggest reject, Jesus loves you with an unwavering love, and that's what He wants us to do also. We are not to judge or condemn another by our own standards or feelings, but to see them through the eyes of love first! If someone is drawn to Christ by our example it will be because they see something in us that appeals to them or they wish they had also. In 1 Corinthians 13:4-13 we read about love. This is an everlasting truth which will prevail for all time. When you read these verses you will see immediately that this is a very different nature to the one we would naturally adopt, yet with the help of the Holy Spirit this is the new nature we are encouraged to live by. No one is pretending these changes in our lives are easy or will necessarily happen overnight, yet if you don't begin to seek and apply the Word of God in your life then you will stagnate and be fruitless for the kingdom.

Hurt of the kind we are discussing causes pain, and pain a distraction; the longer you hold on to it the more it will take over and rule your life. Remember at the beginning of this book we looked at sacrifice and what that meant to Christ, also how it shows us an example of laying down our own lives for others. The longer you nurture your hurt the longer you will not be able to overcome the pain and act upon forgiving others. It's not about excusing what was done to you, but more about wiping the slate clean so that reminder can go away. Remember God said, '*I will remember your sins no more*' (see Hebrews 8:12). That's real forgiveness! Dealing with the issue lifts the burden and frees all involved to the honour of the Lord.

I don't feel I'm in the wrong

You may not be in the wrong, but it would be wrong to do nothing to bring about healing and restoration in the circumstances. It's not so much about the wrong and the right; it's about things more eternal.

In Matthew 16:19 Jesus said to Peter, '*Whatever you bind on earth shall be bound in heaven, and whatever you loose on earth shall be loosed in heaven*' (ESV). Warren Wiersbe says, 'Jesus did not say that God would obey what the disciples did on earth, but they should do on earth what God had already willed. The church does not get man's will done in heaven; it obeys God's will on earth.' In every situation where we have been given responsibility and authority to act in the name of Jesus we will readily see that it comes from the heart of the Father to His will on earth. Why do I share this with you? Because our actions reflect the closeness of our walk with the Lord. The power in forgiveness can be demonstrated clearly when the person suffering from hurt is willing to forgive to glorify the Lord. Actions like these never go unnoticed from heaven. One day God will put to an end those who are against Him, but to those who are faithful He will bless beyond imagination. Forgiving someone may seem like surrender, well, in some way it is; it's surrendering to the will of God allowing Him to work out His purpose in our lives. It's not about how we feel, it's about allowing God to point us in the direction of spiritual maturity; it's about helping us grow deeper in Him.

Let's for a moment think about forgiveness when it involves a person who is not yet a Christian. Do you think that's more of a reason not to forgive? What sort of witness is that to someone who may not understand forgiveness but will only know when it's directed at them? At the core of the message of the gospel is forgiveness of sin. Christ died for sinners not for those who already feel qualified for heaven without repentance; it's not about your feelings once again, it's about your obligation because of the cross of Jesus. I remember a story of a young Christian man who joined the army and declared his Christianity. It wasn't long before he became the object of ridicule simply because he prayed openly in front of his mates and prayed for them. After a while he was set upon and badly hurt. He was back in barracks minding his own business when some of his unit decided to give him a beating to shut him up. At one point the beating was so severe that the young Christian fell and hit his head on the corner of a table, causing a very bad wound. Blood was gushing from the side of his head when one of his unit said to him, 'Why do you persist in telling us about God?' The young man replied, 'I just have to because Jesus died for you and me and shed His blood so that we might be forgiven for our sins and I don't want you to go to hell.'

The young Christian forgave his mates for their actions and became a respected member of his unit for his conviction and testimony.

Whilst we might not feel we are in the wrong, we are being asked to look beyond our own feelings to see the wider picture; that's what God did through Jesus at Calvary. He saw a needy world and found a way to make it possible for us all to respond to an invitation to surrender our lives to Him for a future! Whatever the circumstances around your particular hurt, look beyond to the wider picture and see what God wants to do. Forgiving someone may be the biggest challenge you may face in your Christian journey but, rest assured, it could also have the biggest impact on another's life!

If they have the problem why don't they do something about it?

How easy that would be if everybody else did it for you. Is that what you would like? Do you think the matter would then all be cleared up? What sort of reflection would that be on you, particularly if you are a Christian? There are a number of accounts in scripture where somebody wanted to pass the responsibility on to someone else rather than have to do the task themselves. In Exodus chapters 6 and 7 you see Moses putting up reasons as to why he didn't think either Pharaoh or the people would listen to him. So, what does God do? He gives Moses an aid to work with – Aaron. Even if you don't have an Aaron by your side you have much more as the Holy Spirit promised to be there for you at all times. When you can't do a thing in your strength alone, He is there to guide you and give you the words to minister in the situation.

Remember, it may not be the case that the party causing you a problem is even aware that they have done anything wrong; it's more likely that your conscience is working in you to make the moves first! Put to rest anything that would prevent your fellowship going forward as a Christian and honouring the Lord as we should.

We will always need to be careful how we read a situation, especially if we are going to assume the other party should take the responsibility of putting things right first! John 13:34 is where Jesus says to His disciples, '*A new commandment I give to you, that you love one another*' (NKJV). Certainly not the easiest thing to do when all you want is satisfaction over your pain and hurt. Yet we are still commanded to love one another.

There's a great passage in scripture all about love (1 Corinthians 13). Read this and you will begin to see that without love we have nothing. Remember it was love that nailed the Son of Man to the cross for you and me. As fundamental as this is, it is vital to understand it and apply it to our lives if we are to make a difference.

So, what we are saying is let's be sure who is the one with the burden. A mark of Christian maturity will be shown when we exercise grace in difficult situations, where we put to the back our fleshy and emotional frustrations and allow the calming measure of the Holy Spirit to take over. When you hear today how some parents speak to their children it's no wonder that they don't feel loved. All they know is correction by abuse! Surely it is incumbent on us to set an example to those who need help? Proverbs 11:30 says, '*The fruit of the righteous is a tree of life. And he who wins souls is wise*' (NKJV). It is our job to be wise in the knowledge that God gives us through the working of the Holy Spirit. So, look again – who has the burden? God has given us the privilege to lead by example to show others that love overcomes sin and that strength is found in Him. God's intention is that we should be a blessing to others not a stumbling stone. There is one other point I wish to make in this section regarding why the other party should not necessarily do something first to reconcile a situation. It may be they are just unaware that there is a problem or in fact they themselves are too ashamed to make an approach or too weak to deal with it. This is why the opportunity is there for you to step up and lead the way. It doesn't matter what age you are or what your circumstances are, don't look any longer for an excuse; put love into action and see the way forward by trusting in the Lord.

It wasn't that important anyway

Often problems can be blown up way out of proportion if they are left to fester, that is why we need to keep things in perspective. The longer a situation is allowed to fester the more opportunity for the adversary to corrupt the mind further and prolong a bad situation causing more the loss of reality. Ephesians 4:24 speaks of '[*putting*] *on the new man which was created according to God, in true righteousness and holiness*' (NKJV). It goes on in the following verses to remind us how we should be towards one another, putting away lying and speaking the truth. If things are allowed to fester, the exaggeration over time can develop into a lie – this is not the way for God to be seen in us.

Verses 30-32 sum it up very well where we are commanded not to grieve the Holy Spirit by our misconduct. Many say 'time can be a healer' and in some cases this can be true. However, when there is hurt and pain so dominant as part of the division between two people, time can only cause deeper pain if it's nurtured and not dealt with. If the problem wasn't that important anyway and you allowed it to go on for an unnecessary length of time, have you considered the other person involved or have you just looked inwardly at your own emotional upset? The Bible says be filled with the Spirit. For the Christian this is a command of God; it is not an option. If we are not filled with the Spirit then our lives are not controlled by the Spirit. Therefore, how can we know what is right and wrong unless the Spirit leads us into the truth of God's Word? You may have come to the conclusion that, after time, the problem wasn't that important to you, but consider what time has been wasted if it was something that could easily have been dealt with much sooner? It would be sad to live your life in regret if it became too late to mend the situation, whatever the degree of pain it initially brought. One of the most powerful stories in scripture is the one concerning Joseph (Genesis 37 – 45) who was left for dead by his jealous and angry brothers. Many years later, much to the surprise of the brothers, they find Joseph in high office serving in Pharaoh's courts. They didn't recognise him, but he recognised them.

There came the time when Joseph needed to reveal who he was. The Bible says that Joseph could not restrain himself so he sent everyone out of his presence except his brothers (Genesis 45:1). What happened next was not a show of anger but one of compassion. What Joseph goes on to say was amazing, '*Do not therefore be grieved or angry with yourselves because you sold me here*; *for God sent me before you to preserve life*' (Genesis 45:5 NKJV).

You see, we don't know the ways of the Lord when He has a much bigger plan for our lives; if only we would submit to Him He will reveal the direction He wants us to go. Joseph's brother's left him to the mercy of others or possibly even to die, but God had a bigger plan to preserve them all. How do we know what's important in life when we can only see with our eyes?

CHAPTER EIGHT

WHAT IF IT'S REJECTED?

I can't handle rejection

A good friend of mine, Steve Hepden, has written a book entitled *Rejection Hurts* and I guess the definition for many is in the title. The whole reason we can't handle rejection is that it compounds the hurt that may already exist from unforgiveness. The fear of not knowing if an approach to deal with fellowship breakdown or broken relationships caused by another will work or produce a result. To put it all right can be a huge barrier to some. What if the other person doesn't want to know or will not speak to me, what then? Steve says in his book, 'Rejection is a negative and destructive feeling, which distorts and damages our way of life, undermining our perception of who we are.' You see, if we have a preconceived idea of the outcome of any approach when dealing with sensitive personal issues then we are likely to give up before we have started!

Proverbs 16:3 says, '*Commit your works to the* Lord, *and your thoughts will be established*' (NKJV). Here is the challenge: it's about how we approach the situation that matters. What we have to learn to do is to put our complete trust in the Lord and believe He has gone before us. If your heart is saying there is an issue to put right, then that is by no means an accident! If we are being stirred by the Holy Spirit to do something about a situation then there will be a much bigger and profound reason for us to respond to this call.

Doubtless there is one who will not want you to succeed: the enemy Satan is always there to dissuade you. It is likely your fear of rejection is not there by accident but there as part of the battle that rages whenever Christians are about to respond to the Spirit's call to glorify God. Remember the text says '*your thoughts will be established*'. That means you will be moving in the strength of the Lord and you will be given the right words to say in the situation. If your heart is right and your motives are right then the outcome will also be right.

For those of us who are professing Christians it is essential to understand and know our authority in Christ. Be under no illusion – the moment you make a move towards dealing with a situation from a spiritual standpoint then you have an audience, not of the kind you particularly want but one who is out to try and cause you to stumble and fail. The apostle Paul makes it clear in Ephesians 1:18-23 that we have an inheritance in Christ, we are given power and authority conferred by God. In Colossians 1:29 Paul reminds the church that all our labours are '*striving according to His working which works in [us] mightily*' (NKJV). Paul also says something interesting in Ephesians 3:7: '*I became a minister according to the gift of the grace of God given to me by the effective working of His power*' (NKJV). You see it is not our power but the power of God working through us. We need not fear the enemy who would whisper in our ears that our mission to do the right thing will fail. In Christ we are conquerors. '*He has delivered us from the power of darkness and conveyed us into the kingdom of the Son of His love, in whom we have redemption through His blood, the forgiveness of sins*' (Colossians 1:13-14 NKJV). No longer are we trapped or need we feel defeated before we start to fulfil the work of God.

Rejection is something Christ knew about. '*He is despised and rejected by men, a man of sorrows and acquainted with grief. And we hid, as it were, our faces from Him; He was despised and we did not esteem Him*' (Isaiah 53:3 NKJV). Did Christ turn away from what the Father asked of Him because of rejection? No, He was obedient unto the cross. Nothing was going to change the course and plan of salvation . . . to '*set your minds on things above*' (Colossians 3:2), keep your heart and mind in tune with the Father's will, and go forward in the knowledge that He has gone before you.

I could be wasting my time

The Bible says we should not lean on our own understanding (Proverbs 3:5). If we put our whole trust in the Lord, it says He will direct our paths, He will show us which way to go and what to say.

It may be that the other party doesn't want to be reconciled with you, but this is no excuse not to take the initial steps to be a peacemaker to show that through it all you are going on with the Lord and growing in Him. If you are allowing the Holy Spirit to lead and guide you, there will be a change in your whole outlook when dealing with other people. So many of us would rather hide and go in the other direction than to face up to the conviction that something has to happen and it has to happen in me first of all. The Bible says, '*Blessed are the peacemakers, for they shall be called the children of God*' (Matthew 5:9). This is where compassion and mercy come into play; again not our natural characteristics necessarily, but essential if we are to see the working of God in our lives.

The key to seeing a change in many circumstances may have to begin in us. It is not our business to go around expecting to change people because we have had a revelation about putting a situation right, and it's certainly not within our remit to try and convert people because we feel it makes us feel better for our actions. Firstly, let the change take place in us, let our attitude and outlook change to reflect what God wants to do in us by the precious Holy Spirit. You will never be wasting your time if you are acting in accordance with the guidance of the Holy Spirit. If you are led by the Holy Spirit and you are obedient in responding to what the Spirit of God is telling you to do you will not be wasting your time. Our problem is often that we want to see immediate results! Think back: did everything in your life have immediate results? Probably not. But that doesn't mean we don't wait or leave it to the Lord. We can't forget that God's agenda for dealing with all men is uniquely His. So it's only right that once we have responded to the Word of God, we leave it to Him to perform the miracle that has to take place. It's for His glory not ours. I am so thankful that God didn't waste His time seeking me out to respond to His Word and call on my life to follow Him; even when I wasn't listening, He didn't give up on me. Praise the Lord, and He won't give up on you. You will not waste a moment of your time if you give your whole being over to the Lord who will fulfil His plan for your life.

Not in my strength

The wonderful thing about God is He doesn't need help from people who feel they have something to give to the giver of all things! We have already seen in previous pages that God chooses the weak things in this life to accomplish the greatest tasks. For many of us we have to get to this stage of realising that when all else is exhausted then we need to let go and let God show us a better way. Wonderful words in John 14 where Jesus comforts His disciples. They had a number of questions that needed answers and Jesus sums it up beautifully in verse 6: '*I am the way and the truth and the life. No one comes to the Father except through me.*' What Jesus is saying is there is only one way to God and it's through Him; God is holy and only those who have a great High Priest (Jesus) can have access to Him. It's because our life is hid in Christ, we are made acceptable by His righteousness. The truth of this word is borne out in the new life we have in Jesus when we surrender our lives to Him. At that moment the Holy Spirit indwells us to confirm the promises of God in our lives. Verse 12 of John 14 says, '*He that believeth on me, the works that I do shall he do also; and greater works than these shall he do*' (KJV). If Jesus is saying we can do the works He did as well as greater things, then why would we need our own strength to do the works of God. God has commissioned us to carry on the works that He would have done had He not returned to the Father. The power that is given to men is to glorify God and when we pray in the Spirit for God to move in miraculous ways, He has promised to answer. Even in weakness we are made strong, learning to depend on God is vital to the effectiveness of our ministry in serving God at all levels.

Isaiah 40:29 says, '*He gives strength to the weary and increases the power of the weak.*' This is the provision of God especially to those who are weak. It's not easy to come to terms with the fact that our strength is not always enough to deal with every situation, especially when we are called to deal with spiritual matters. Realising we need to depend on God to provide the strength we need, brings us closer to him. The following verses 30 and 31 should be our encouragement as we wait upon the Lord.

When David confronted Goliath in 1 Samuel 17 it wasn't David's strength compared to the giant of Goliath that put David off from the duel that was about to take place, because David went to battle in the strength of the Lord. When Moses got to the Red Sea, it wasn't his strength or power that would part the waves, but that of the Lord. When God asks us to do something, He doesn't ask us to do it in our strength. He has promised to provide us with all the power we need to do His will. There is power in forgiveness because it demonstrates God's power in us equipping us to do His will. The apostle Paul says in Philippians 4:13, '*I can do all this through him who gives me strength.*' Paul is saying, in all circumstances, I can do everything that is required of me because of God's provision of strength. We are not asked to apply our strength in spiritual situations but trust in the Lord. Isaiah 41:10 is a promise of God that cannot be broken and should encourage every believer when going through challenging times: '*Fear not, for I am with you; be not dismayed, for I am your God. I will strengthen you, yes, I will help you, I will uphold you with My righteous right hand*' (NKJV). No matter how big the problem, no matter how difficult the issue, God is with us. This is all made possible because of the greatness of the Lord. A number of times in this chapter God says *'Fear not'* meaning put your trust in Him, be confident that He has already made a way. He will guide us on the right path to lead us to the place of restoration and healing. No longer a case of 'Not in my strength' but a revelation of all things in His strength and power, making the impossible possible.

CHAPTER NINE

WHERE DOES LOVE COME INTO FORGIVENESS?

Once again, we need to be reminded of how we should respond given difficult situations, and in particular when we need to show forgiveness.

The reason we have entered into a relationship with Christ is because He first loved us and we responded to His call upon our lives. The Bible reminds us that when we accepted Christ as our Saviour we actually asked Him to come in and dwell with us. The moment we did this the precious Holy Spirit became a part of us and therefore our lives are no longer our own; we are asking for help to be guided and set on a right course in which to glorify God in our lives. We may never know how much God loves us unless we get close to Him and fellowship with Him.

It is said that you become the person you are by the influence of those around you. In other words, mix with the wrong sort and you may pay heavy consequences for your behaviour and actions. Some years ago I met a man who had been brought up in the world of drugs and alcohol, his father was deeply entrenched in the drug world in London and all this man knew as a youth was a corrupt and dark world of lives not meaning much as long as they could survive on the money made through this terrible business.

Because of this the man spent the early years of his life in prison on more than a few occasions. Sometime later he was attending an Alcoholics Anonymous meeting when he met a lady who later became his wife. They both made a conscious decision to give up their past life and start over anew. You could say he found love and realised that there was more to life than the life he had known. So it is with us; when Christ comes in, new life begins. Some of the hallmarks will be evident in the way we live. Ephesians 4:31-32 says, *'Get rid of all bitterness, rage and anger, brawling and slander, along with every form of malice. Be kind and compassionate to one another, forgiving each other just as in Christ God forgave you.'* May I encourage you to seek the instruction for your life from God's Word, not to read the Bible like a novel or some casual reading, but as an essential part of your daily diet as the bread of life.

My own personal experience in learning to forgive started many years ago when in the early years of my life my mother and father split up, leaving 5 children without a mother. To compound this, in a very short space of time we found ourselves in an orphanage 60 miles away from our father who couldn't look after us as well as keep his job. This is going back to the late 50s, early 60s. I didn't know what rejection and abandonment was all about at the time, but over the years it became painfully obvious. To further compound the separation, the home we were in would dictate when Dad could come to visit and normally visiting was once a month. It was very hard to see Dad for a few hours on visiting day and all of us get the attention we needed.

At the time we entered the home I wasn't a Christian, nevertheless the home was built on Christian principles and so we were expected to attend church every Sunday morning, afternoon and sometimes evening. Even then I still didn't feel a need to make a commitment to Christ. A few years later I attended a crusade in Bristol and heard the gospel message in a way I had never heard it before. I was told by the preacher that Jesus died for all our hurts and pain as well as our sin that needed God's forgiveness for us to have eternal life. I remember the occasion well; as the service came to an end and the choir sang the song 'Just As I Am Without One Plea' I realised the love of Jesus was drawing me to Himself. The man who led me to the Lord was a lovely godly man who graciously and gently showed me the purpose of the cross and why Jesus died for me. I accepted Jesus as my Lord and Saviour and that was when my journey started. All of a sudden I was aware I was not fatherless; even though my earthly dad could not be there for me most of the time, my heavenly Father was always there from that moment on. There were plenty of times in the years before this I felt unloved, deserted, sometimes forgotten and totally confused about all that was happening around me and my siblings. But now there was a new experience that was about to carry me through a very winding path going forward.

An earlier episode in my life should have also impacted me in a negative way. This was when I was sexually assaulted by a neighbour who was well known to the family, and then a second time when I was visiting a landmark in Bristol, waiting for my dad to come out of work. On each occasion I didn't understand what was going on. I was no more than 10 years old at the time. I could not talk about these occurrences for nearly 30 years. When I came to terms with what had happened I felt very hurt, resentful and let down. I didn't know who to blame or what to blame, all I knew was the pain didn't go away. One of the persons responsible threatened that if I ever told anybody about what had happened, something horrible would come my way – that stuck for years. When I became a Christian, it took some years of teaching before I was able to start to address these issues in my life.

One of the pivotal moments was when I heard others give their testimonies of similar happenings and how they got over the pain and hurt. These were people who had put their trust in Jesus as Lord and Saviour, whose lives had been changed and were able to move forward. Part of the solution was to forgive the people who had hurt me, even if they were no longer alive. Because all will stand before the judgement throne of God to be judged one day for how we spent our time on earth before Jesus returns. Is it possible that either of these men might have come to Jesus as their Lord and Saviour also? It's not for me to judge or condemn them. This is God's business and His alone.

What happened then is now in the past. I feel no hurt nor anger but sadness for what might be lost souls. I needed to forgive to be free of the thing that constantly held me back and prevented me from the joy that God intended in my life when coming to Him. Love is a major part of our recovery in forgiveness. As mentioned before, without love we have nothing.

I was also at that place where I needed to forgive my dad for putting us in an orphanage. I didn't realise how much that had subconsciously affected me as I was growing up. I remember the day: I was convicted of the Lord to go and talk to my dad and tell him my feelings and how I tried to understand why things had happened the way they did;

most of all was to tell him I loved him. Rarely had he told us as children that he loved us, but that didn't stop me needing to tell him. All because of Jesus.

My father was a fairly quiet person who usually kept his feelings to himself. I wanted him to know that I held a resentment towards him for being sent to an orphanage. I harboured this for years without realising the consequence that made it difficult for me to express my love for him. When we were able to talk, he explained how difficult it was for him to work and at the same time bring up a family on a very low wage. He also said that he personally had very sad days due to the separation. Sadly, I had only thought of my own feelings and not his. I found myself asking God to forgive me for my selfishness and blindness in the situation. I knew my dad found it difficult to tell us that he loved us but I believe he did; this was borne out when I went to tell him I loved him. I thank God for opening my eyes to things around me to take away burdens we don't need to carry.

If love is not a part of forgiveness how can we forgive and really mean it? The love we are talking about is the love that shows a right and genuine attitude towards those who may have caused us pain.

Ephesians 4:24 commends us to '*put on the new man which was created according to God, in righteousness and holiness*' (NKJV). At the end of the chapter it reminds us not to grieve the Holy Spirit but to '*be kind to one another, tender hearted, forgiving one another, even as God in Christ forgave you*' (NKJV). If we are walking in the Spirit because the Spirit is in us, then surely this is because our lives are given over to the Spirit to control our actions, thoughts and deeds.

Love seals the deal

Normally, it's true to say we don't go around looking to hurt people or to cause harm in any way, although our sinful self might disagree, especially if we have been hurt by someone else. It may be difficult to love someone who has caused so much pain and hurt, but this is no reason to perpetuate the situation. We are talking about a life that is stuck in the world without any sense of direction or hope. God's love for us is so great He makes it stick for eternity. He found a way to show the whole world how much He loves us and made a way through the cross and the sacrifice of Jesus to seal the deal. God said if we confess our sins, He is faithful and just to forgive us of our sins. God provided a way that demands action on our part to respond to His call on our life. The action on our part is to enter into an eternal relationship with Him; the only way possible is by the cross of Calvary and giving our lives over to Him.

Now we are directly in fellowship with the Father through the Son. What's more is that God loves us with an everlasting love that cannot be broken or taken away. '*Who shall separate us from the love of Christ? Shall tribulation, or distress, or persecution, or famine, or nakedness, or peril, or sword?*' (Romans 8:35 NKJV). It seems clear to me that nothing can rob us of the knowledge and joy of knowing Jesus; we are loved with an everlasting love. I believe this is an amazing fact that should be uppermost in anyone's testimony.

Many years ago I spent a short time in a soup kitchen in Edinburgh, Scotland. I was in my early twenties and had never experienced a situation like this before. The soup kitchen was down a back street in what seemed to be a

Dickensian type of building, not very well kept, a bit musty and all a bit tired. The scene that welcomed me has stuck with me ever since. I entered a large open space where the walls were showing the signs of age with damp penetrating the inner surface; the floor was wooden boarded and well worn; long, wooden tables and benches filled the available space. At the front of the room and adjacent to a small kitchen a large table was arrayed with metal cooking pots steaming with hot soup and food which was ready to be distributed to the many needy folk who had come in and occupied every available space.

What surprised me was the age range. It seemed to span from the very young to the older generation. The one thing in common was their need of help, all eagerly hunched over their bowls devouring their food as if it was the last meal they might get. I found this so hard to comprehend, particularly in this day and age and in this country. My host told me some of the stories behind the faces. Some had nowhere to live, some had succumbed to drink and drugs as a result of falling on hard times. People who were in professions and had come through broken marriages and emotional upsets and could no longer cope with life. What really spoke to me was the few people who served those in need. There was no judgement on each individual or their situation, just a desire to want to serve them and share the love of Jesus. This service was extended onto the streets at night by the same people, seeking out those who were in need.

This demonstrates a heart of love – no judgement but a desire to honour God by sharing a love that can change lives.

There was no distinction or separation between those who served and those who needed serving. It was clear that to want to work in a place like this you needed compassion for those you were helping. It was also obvious that the Christian workers loved what they were doing; they showed a real love for those they served. I came away from this place realising that if I was to serve the Lord, I needed a similar attitude – one of compassion – a love that was non-judgemental and a forgiving spirit no matter what I knew about these people. Sometimes it's not easy to serve others when they return abuse or insults or spit at you because you want to help them and you want to share Jesus with them. Not everybody that receives the love and hospitality that is handed out reciprocates naturally. Many will feel it's the duty of the more fortunate to serve them in this way. Sadly some are very difficult to satisfy – they throw the food on the floor because somebody has a bigger helping, they can often cause more trouble and disrupt the whole situation – but you ask yourself if that is a reason not to pursue what God has asked you to do in His name. It's not so difficult to see how love and forgiveness work together.

Another thing regarding the soup kitchen: it was not on the high street, it did not have a shop front to advertise what was going on behind the façade, but it quietly fulfilled a vital service to those in need as a place of refuge and a safe place where the friends serving could be trusted. On the other hand, it could have been on the high street with a big shop front and big sign advertising what went on. The success of this ministry within the city was because it was where it was: it didn't embarrass those who needed to go there, it was not an intimidating place where these needy folks felt they couldn't enter even if they were desperate for a meal. Here was a quiet work being done to serve and honour God so that all the glory went to Him. Sometimes we are asked to do things without being seen by the world at large. Matthew 6:1 reminds us that we must have a right heart and motive to do works that are not seen by others to show that our motive is to bring glory to God alone. It's the same when we are led to forgive someone; there is no need to make a public spectacle concerning our actions.

Going the extra step

How many of us in the past have said when asked to do something, OK, I'll do it but don't ask me to do it or anything else again. Going the extra step may be the difference between success and failure. It's not recorded that Jesus counted each step of the journey from Jerusalem to Calvary although He felt the pain of each one; He did it for you and for me.

We have already talked about the sacrifice of giving, going the extra step comes into the same category. If we believe our lives are no longer our own when we come to Christ as Lord and Saviour, then it is much more about how we are led going forward. When Moses led the children of Israel out of Egypt, they had to endure a number of extra steps before reaching the promised land.

How they grumbled and moaned, and yet what was not too obvious to them was God wanted to teach them to learn to trust Him now they were no longer in bondage to slavery. In a similar way we too are asked to go the extra step, taking us out of our comfort zone to unchartered territory spiritually to experience putting our whole trust in God.

Galatians 5:13-25 speaks of how we can begin to move in the Spirit. It speaks of serving one another humbly, in love; it speaks of walking in the Spirit. The gospel songwriter Don Moen wrote a song entitled 'God Will Make a Way'. The question is, do we believe this is possible for us, especially when we know we need to put things right, but not to do it in our strength, because God will make a way? Verse 25 of the chapter says, '*Since we live by the Spirit, let us keep in step with the Spirit.*' By walking in the Spirit we will not fulfil the desires of the flesh, we won't be relying on our own strength in situations that need the understanding, sensitivity and tenderness of the Holy Spirit. When we allow the Holy Spirit to guide us then the supernatural can take place.

Jesus' parable of the Good Samaritan is a great example of one who went the extra mile. It was not about race or class; it was about someone in need and addressing that need. He could have stopped, made a token gesture and moved on, but this didn't happen. He went the extra steps to ensure the one who was in need had their need met. So it is with those who need our forgiveness. It's about seeing beyond the problem enough to exercise the love of Jesus. How can the cost of the extra step be so great that we should ignore it? Jesus used this example to teach the religious leaders of the day a simple lesson. Love your neighbour, whoever they are, especially if they are in need.

It's reasonable to say that stepping out of our comfort zone is not the most attractive thing to do, particularly when we are asked to go into unfamiliar territory. '*The steps of a good man are ordered by the LORD, and He delights in his way. Though he fall, he shall not be utterly cast down; for the LORD upholds him with His hand*' (Psalm 37:23-24).

These verses talk about someone who is strong and yet needs the Lord to guide and support him in any situation, even when his steps have been set out and his journey prepared. God provides all we need even when we fall. As long as we are in step with the Spirit of God, we will know God's provision and protection in all we do for Him. There are times when we will stumble but this is not defeat or final; God's plan is to protect His children and set us on our way again. He is a God of restoration and continuation for our lives as we do His will.

No matter what is ahead of us God has gone before us to prepare the way. Yes, even when we are asked to move out of our comfort zones and do something for Him. There is no peace in running away from problems, that just delays the outcome.

When it comes to forgiveness it need not be a battle but a breakthrough. *'Do not withhold good from those to whom it is due, when it is in the power of your hand to do so'* (Proverbs 3:27 NKJV). We are called to make a difference no matter where we live or who lives around us, it's simply by example. Nothing comes without patience, prayer and wisdom if we are to see a move of God in our lives, our neighbourhood or place of work.

A reassuring aspect of serving the Lord is knowing He is right there in the situation no matter what. Remember God does not make promises He cannot keep; He will see us through. This life's journey may be made up of a series of extra steps but all lead to the same outcome: a closer walk with God for all who are obedient enough to do His will. There's an old hymn we used to sing which has in the first verse the words to express confidence in the Lord;

All the way my Saviour leads me –
What have I to ask beside?
Can I doubt His tender mercy?
Who through life has been my guide?
Heavenly peace, divinest comfort,
Here by faith in Him to dwell!
For I know whate'er befall me,
Jesus doeth all things well.

Taking extra steps can be daunting, especially when they are steps of faith. But how are we expected to grow if we don't do what has been made available to us with all the promises of God alongside? I hear people say, I wish I had done this or that in days gone by but I feel it's too late now. When it comes to forgiveness it's never too late for us to act. People can be dying spiritually because they have resolved it is too late to act. Don't let your past or your fear of the future stop you from entering into a deeper experience of knowing God and allowing the Holy Spirit to bring you to a new place on your journey.

Remember our life is hid in Christ, we are safe in His care and control, He has promised to guide us through, right to the very end – not to be disappointed but to receive the reward He has for us one day.

CHAPTER TEN

ALL BECAUSE HE FORGAVE ME

Why did I need forgiving in the first place?

It is essential that we understand a fundamental truth from scripture. It says in Hebrews 9:22, *'Without the shedding of blood there is no forgiveness.'* Plainly, if Jesus had not gone to the cross for you and me there would not have been a way that was acceptable to God for the forgiveness of our sin. I hear you say, 'But I am a good person, I haven't done anything wrong, I haven't disobeyed the Law, so why do I need to be forgiven? I am not a sinner.'

The Bible says that all have fallen short of the glory of God (Romans 3:23). Jesus says to a man named Nicodemus in John 3:3, *'No one can see the kingdom of God unless they are born again.'* Romans 3:10 spells it out so clearly: without forgiveness of sin we cannot be saved, we are still separated from God. There were many and still are those who think service will be their way to heaven. The Bible states that without repentance we remain in our sinful state (Luke 13:3). In a world that is heading for disaster, a world that never seems to learn from wars, a world where there is so much poverty, a world where the classes seem to be further and further apart, now is the time if ever before we need a Saviour. There seems to be understanding that the message of the gospel is more relevant today than ever before. Even in a sinful state a holy God will hear the cry of a repentant sinner crying out for help. John 1:12 says receiving Christ as your Saviour is the beginning of knowing forgiveness in your life; being born again is what God does for you. This is the new birth, a miracle of spiritual life where the Holy Spirit of God indwells you. Now we are no longer on our own, nor are we in control anymore. Repentance is to submit ourselves to God who takes control if we let Him. Again, without forgiveness we cannot be saved. Is this not a good enough reason to ask God for His forgiveness so that our lives can be transformed by the Holy Spirit's power to glorify Him?

Part of the wonderful ministry of the Holy Spirit is to bring us to a place of understanding. Once a need has been identified, then the work to meet and satisfy that need is where we can seek help from the Holy Spirit to guide us along the path to resolving the need.

In the first instance it's about hearing the Word of God, which may not come only through the written word or spoken word but through the power of the Holy Spirit speaking to our hearts. The promise of God is when we truly seek Him, we will find Him. Just in the same way Jesus says, '*Very truly, I tell you, whoever hears my word and believes him who has sent me has eternal life and will not be judged but has crossed over from death to life*' (John 5:24). What God is offering us is a relationship from now unto eternity; it's all about getting closer to Him as a loving Father. James 4:8 says, '*Draw near to God and He will draw near to you*' (NKJV). Once we are in covenant with God from heaven's point of view this is an unbreakable arrangement. Once I have exercised my faith towards becoming the person God wants me to be, the resources of heaven are at my disposal. The problem occurs when we don't take what is on offer to us, we choose often to do it our way and choose not to avail ourselves of all the spiritual help, food and instruction that is found in the Word of God. We need to be reminded that unforgiveness is a barrier or separation from God; He is Holy and cannot look upon sin. This is why Jesus came. He was the propitiation for our sin; it was through His sacrifice at Calvary that made it possible for us to be made acceptable to God. We know it cost Jesus His life for us to be right and acceptable to God and it means action on our part to embrace our salvation and start living a life that reflects the love of Christ in a dark world today. I know that throughout this book I have seemingly repeated myself, but I make no apology for stating the truth found in the Word of God. I remember as a young Christian we were taught that the Bible is our handbook for life. I am glad God saw it necessary to make this known to us no matter what age, the words and wisdom are ageless.

Does it mean once and forever?

When a person asks God to forgive them of their sins in true repentance He will do so because He has promised through His Word to do so and He is a covenant-making God not a covenant-breaking God. I am so glad that from a young age I was taught that when Jesus died on the cross He did a complete work, it was once and for all. Sometimes a problem occurs when we think we may have committed the unforgivable sin or we think our sin is too great to be forgiven. Jesus bore the sins of the world, not just yours and mine but the whole world's sin. What use would Calvary have been if it was only for a selective number of sins? The Bible reminds us that God's desire is that none should perish or spend an eternity lost from the love and fellowship with Him.

There are those folks who think that they have committed the unforgivable sin and this is their reason for not seeking forgiveness and pardon from the Lord. The fact that you are mindful of the situation means all is not lost. If you have committed the unforgivable sin then there would be no continued desire to try and put things right, your heart would be as stone. In Matthew 12:31-32 Jesus says, *'Therefore I say to you, every sin and blasphemy will be forgiven men, but the blasphemy against the Spirit will not be forgiven men. Anyone who speaks a word against the Son of Man, it will be forgiven him; but whoever speaks against the Holy Spirit, it will not be forgiven him, either in this age or in the age to come'* (NKJV). The ministry of the Holy Spirit is so important in the conviction and also the conversion of the soul that no one can be saved without the Holy Spirit working in our lives. Shut out the Holy Spirit and you lose fellowship with God. Our problem is we sometimes want to grade sin; we deceive ourselves by thinking one sin is greater than the other. Outside of the sin described above, all other sin is forgivable, yes, even murder, blasphemy, theft and adultery. God is saying to us that if we know we have sinned then come and seek forgiveness for that sin and get right with God. God will not turn you away if you seek after Him and He will forgive a repentant sinner.

A gift that has to be shared

How many of us when we receive a gift take it, hide it away purely so you and you alone can enjoy it? I'm sure not all are this way but it's true to say those who rarely get gifts may react in this way. I can remember my own children when they were young how they loved opening their gifts at Christmas or on their birthdays, how their eyes would light up especially if it was the gift that they were hoping for. Generally, they had to have time when they would just enjoy the gift alone and then after time they would want to show and share this enjoyment with others.

The scripture tells us that God gives us only good gifts whether they are for us personally or gifts that are to be shared (Matthew 7:11). For those who love the Lord the Bible tells us to 'desire spiritual gifts' (1 Corinthians 14:1 NKJV). There is a prerequisite for seeking spiritual gifts and this is found in 1 Corinthians 13 – it says without love we have nothing. This again is the same strong reason for adopting the attitude of Christ when He walked this earth and ministered to the lost. Again, it is said that when Jesus bore our sins on the cross it was love that nailed Him to the cross, a love that was an example for us to follow when we are called to come out of our comfort zones and use the gift that God has given us through His Son. How can I not share this gift of love with others and show forgiveness if that's what I have personally experienced through Christ my Saviour? Don't think that if you have received a gift like this you can be selective in how you use it. God has called us to love our neighbours, our enemies and one another. Our priority is to share this gift to all the world; whether they receive it or not, is not our concern. No matter what you have in this world, whether you are rich or poor, we are commanded to share. We forget that every good thing we have is provided by God. *'Command them to do good, to be rich in good deeds, and to be generous and willing to share'* (1 Timothy 6:18-19). Jesus said, *'It is more blessed to give than to receive'* (Acts 20:35). Well, there is immense pleasure in giving, especially when you see the good that can come from it.

I can testify to the goodness of God when I have been prompted over the years to give something away rather than sell it. I have never been left without. On one occasion my wife and I decided to help another member of our family out by giving away our electric cooker. It went to a home where there was much need for the item. We didn't have much money at the time but felt this was the right course of action to take. It meant that we would have to go and buy another cooker for ourselves, so we went to the shop, only this time we couldn't afford to buy one so we had to take out finance for the purchase through the shop. We were told we would have to sign some papers in a few days' time to complete the purchase. The day came when the shop rang me at my place of work and asked me to go with my wife to complete the purchase. We were greeted by the sales assistance who told us the manager wanted to see us in his office. Naturally we were somewhat perplexed, thinking our application had been refused. On entering the manager's office he walked towards us to shake our hands and told us that because we were the 100,000th customer to purchase goods in the shop from the time they opened, our purchase was to be given to us free of charge! God is a faithful God; He saw the whole scenario played out just as He planned it.

There were many other occasions I could account for where seemingly the impossible was possible for God.

In my early 20s the gospel group we formed was invited to West Germany for 3 weeks to minister at a youth conference. Following this experience my wife and I were invited back for a year to work with an evangelist, Willi Buchwald, who worked for the New Life Evangelistic Organisation. I gave up my job with the architectural practice I worked for and my wife gave up her job. The time spent in Germany was an eye opener and taught us many things, not least to trust God for each day as we went with no financial guarantee of money from one day to the next. When the year was up we returned to England to find work, a home and the means on which to live. Within the first week of our return we needed somewhere to live, we had very little money and no food.

We managed to secure our first house with help from the parents-in-law. I remember in the first week we ran out of money and didn't want to ask the family to support us further. I prayed and asked the Lord to provide our needs. The following morning I heard a knock at the front door and went to open the door to find a large box on the door step. I took the box in to show my wife and when we opened it we found enough food provisions for a week. We asked around the family as to who had kindly given us this gift. Nobody knew anything about it. To this day I do not know who was so kind, but what I do know is that God is faithful – He knew what was needed and arranged for someone to share with us. A few days later a friend turned up at our door and handed me some keys to a very new mini-van and said that the Lord had told him that there was a need and to give the vehicle to us.

When we went to Germany for the year, we gave our furniture away and sold other items to provide the money for travel, all of which in the human sense would not make any sense at all. But when God asks you to do something, maybe out of the ordinary, don't be surprised when He has covered every possible avenue to ensure you are provided for then and now. God will never leave us without; He always provides our needs. When you are asked by the Lord to share, don't do it thinking 'what will I get out of it?' but do it to honour God who is bountiful in goodness. I love the scripture where it says He will supply our needs (Philippians 4:19). What I think I want is not necessarily what I really need. What is amazing, often what I have is only on loan until the Lord says, 'Now give it away,' or 'Share what I have given you.'

Remember, God sees the bigger picture, He knows when and where help is most needed. Learning to listen and respond in this matter is just as important as knowing when we need to forgive someone else, all of which is to bring glory to the Lord.

CHAPTER ELEVEN

WHEN HEALING COMES

The wider picture

It has never failed to amaze me that when God brings about healing in any situation, it can often have a much bigger and wider impact than we would otherwise have thought. We often think of healing as purely a bodily need, but the Bible reminds us that we also have spiritual needs. We live in an age where stress and mental health are high on the personal agenda of many people who find it difficult to manage even the most menial tasks due to a physical or mental condition preventing them from leading what would otherwise be considered a normal life. So it is with the spiritual life. We can be held back from the enjoyment of life to the full simply because something has overwhelmed us spiritually. Just as I mentioned in the previous chapter, God has a bigger plan for blessing even when it seems to be for an individual need. So it is when it comes to spiritual needs being met.

The problem is we can't see the bigger picture from God's point of view. We see the immediate and are often handicapped because that's all we can see. The Bible says, 'Trust in the LORD with all your heart, and lean not on your *own understanding*' (Proverbs 3:5). It's more about putting our trust in an all-powerful, all-knowing God, who is able to bring a greater blessing than we could possibly imagine.

The meaning of healing is 'the process of making or becoming sound or healthy again'. So, the two types of healing we are looking at are physical healing and spiritual healing. It's interesting to note that both can become intrinsic to the other; often when spiritual healing comes so it is with a manifestation in the body which also becomes whole or healthy again. From the Christian's point of view, we need to be aware that the powerful work of the Holy Spirit is availed in such cases. Our joy is to be part of a much bigger plan or blessing when we let the Lord take control.

Perhaps for most we are not so good at letting someone else take control. This can simply be because we want to be in control and not to be dictated to or led by anyone else. But in the case of forgiveness we need to come to a clear understanding that we don't have the answers to all that life is about, we only know in part, and that may be due to our limited experience.

Leaving a lasting legacy

Now is the time we have no other course but to put our complete trust in the Lord. He is able, He is just and merciful towards those who seek after Him and walk in His ways. There is a responsibility on us to leave a lasting legacy that will not only impact a life but will possibly change a life with the guidance and help of the Holy Spirit. If by your surrender to the will of God and a heart of forgiveness you minister according to God's plan then expect to see a miracle in the life of another. It's not necessarily about waiting around to see the result of your obedience; it's all about you being prepared for what the Lord has ahead for you. Don't think because you don't see the result of your actions that it's all forgotten. God is still in control and the glory is all due to Him. Left to our own devices we may well have caused more harm than good in a situation simply because we tried to do things our way. Leaving a legacy is about leaving something to benefit another as we previously discussed. Let your actions be those that show your life being surrendered to a greater and higher authority. You can either leave a trail of destruction as you journey through life trying to do things by yourself or you can leave a pathway for others leading to the cross of Jesus, a place where life itself can be completely changed for all eternity. Psalm 144:15 says, '*Happy is that people, whose God is the Lord*' (KJV). By your example others will realise that our trust is in the Lord, that by the way you live others will see your dependence is in Him. When we become a member of the family of God His provision in all situations abounds towards us. He lifts us up when we are bowed down, He picks us up when we fall, He opens our eyes when we need to see the things that matter around us, and much more.

If someone asks you what you would like to leave as a legacy in this world, what would you say? It may be you don't have much in the way of money or possessions, but ask yourself is this the best you have to offer? Some of the poorest people on earth are in fact the richest, particularly if they have given their lives over to God. We forget when we come to Christ as our personal Saviour that we become heirs to the throne of grace; we have an inheritance that can also be the same for all who humble themselves and bow the knee to Christ. Being forgiven is an amazing gift of God, forgiving someone else is a wonderful gift to pass on. As we forgive, we honour God, we also remove the obstacle that hinders the Holy Spirit from working in us to God's glory. So much of this world has a price on it, but to forgive is priceless, the value of which you will never know, but the legacy you leave will be such a testimony to others.

All glory and power is His

Without a Saviour we cannot know God and have fellowship with Him; without faith we cannot please God. In our sinful state we cannot glory in the Saviour who died for us and who longed for us to receive of Him all the goodness of a loving Father. It's true to say that if left to our imagination we often see things so far removed from reality. It's also true to say that the power of the mind can produce the wrong interpretation and can cause unnecessary pain; if we put our trust in God, a greater power to lead and guide us, we undoubtedly will know His presence beside us. Many lives have been lost down through the ages simply because they didn't know the love of Jesus, they hadn't realised they had a purpose in living and living a righteous life. The message of the gospel of Jesus Christ is that He came into the world to save the lost and make a way back to God through the shedding of His precious blood on the cross of Calvary. He was the perfect sacrifice for the sins of the world. What was Calvary all about? Forgiveness. We need to be forgiven for the wrongs we have done whether we are the one who has been wronged or whether we are the one harbouring unforgiveness.

Let's talk about Jesus. He came to show us all with a clear purpose the plan of salvation. There was a need to come and deal with the state of humanity. '*I have not come to call the righteous, but sinners to repentance*' (Luke 5:32). How often do you go into a church and hear the gospel message preached without the consequence of sin also being explained? We don't receive salvation through service or excusing ourselves by some estimation of our own righteousness. If this were the case, we would not need a Saviour. '*This is a faithful saying and worthy of all acceptance, that Christ Jesus came into the world to save sinners*' (1 Timothy 1:15 KJV). This is the plan of salvation; Jesus came to do what no other human being could do in his own strength. Jesus reminds us that no one person can come to the Father except through Him – He is the way.

The Bible clearly shows us that salvation is the only way back to God, to know and fellowship with Him. Jesus paid the ultimate price for this at Calvary; what should have been our punishment became His sacrifice for you and me. We talked about this earlier in the book, but it bears repeating because of the importance of all we do and all we become either with Christ as our Saviour or if we decide to reject the gift of salvation that has been made available to us. The Bible says in 1 John 5:12, '*He who has the Son has life; he who does not have the Son of God does not have life*' (NKJV). There's no half-way house, if you want to know that your future is secure in Jesus then you have to make a decision. Am I for Christ or not? It seems we live in a world that is getting worse by the day concerning our love for others; there seems to be a wider gap in the classes, typified by the poverty we see around us as well as those who live to become richer by the minute. Is this really what life is all about? When Jesus says He came to seek the lost, there is something quite profound in the meaning of this when you consider what it's about. The Bible speaks clearly about 'the lost', the whole purpose of Jesus being born into this world was to save people from their sins. Without Christ we are lost.

When we come to Christ and accept Him as Lord and Saviour, we are transformed into the new life God intended for us. That means there is a reason to glorify Him by the amazing transformation that takes place in us. A number of Christians haven't yet woken up to the realisation of the newness of life found in Christ, often because they expect to sit back and do nothing but wait for His coming. The great commission to the disciples is extended to us to go into the world and preach the gospel of Jesus Christ, to let the world know there is another way. If we haven't received forgiveness ourselves then why would we imagine we should forgive anybody else. Jesus came to redeem the world from sin (Titus 2:14) to put right what was wrong.

Forgiveness is putting right what is wrong, it becomes a release from burdens we don't have to carry any longer. Unless we have the example of Christ where would we be but subject to man's weak interpretation of what this life is all about. I have prayed for many people through my Christian life and the greatest privilege is to know and see the hand of God at work in a repentant sinner; it's as if until that moment they didn't realise there was any hope beyond this life. One of the most powerful moments is to see and hear a new-born Christian telling others of their experience when knowing their sins need no longer be accounted against them. I guess it's like someone who has been accused of some crime being forgiven and set free – just imagine. We can forgive someone but we can't change their life with a lasting purpose – that is the precious work of the Holy Spirit – but we are privileged to be part of that person's journey in faith. Giving God the glory is to praise and honour His name and acknowledge all that He is in us and for us. When we humble ourselves we acknowledge a higher authority, one who rules over us in love, grace and mercy. Let the forgiveness shown to us be the supreme example of us demonstrating the love towards others who may have caused us harm or ill of some kind. GIVE GOD THE GLORY.